PAUL SELIGSON
TOM ABRAHAM
CRIS GONTOW

English ID

2nd edition

Workbook 1

Richmond

ID Language map

	Question syllabus	Vocabulary	Grammar	Speaking & Skills
1	1.1 Are you Canadian?	Countries & nationalities Adjectives (opinion)	Verb *be* (Present)	Give opinions
	1.2 How do you spell your last name?	Numbers 1–10		Introduce yourself
	1.3 What's your email address?	Personal objects (singular & plural)	Demonstrative pronouns	
	1.4 Are these your glasses?	Adjectives & colors	Possessive adjectives	
	1.5 What's your full name?	Greetings		Give personal information
2	2.1 When do you get up?	Days of the week Time *go to* (*a* / *the* / —)		Talk about routine
	2.2 What do you do in the mornings?	Morning routine	Simple present ⊕ ⊖	Describe your morning routine
	2.3 Who do you live with?	Family	Simple present *Wh-* ❓	Answer personal information questions
	2.4 When do you check your phone?	Frequency adverbs Cell phone verbs		Talk about how often you do things
	2.5 How do you celebrate your birthday?	Special occasions	Frequency adverbs	Process personal information
3	3.1 What's the weather like?	Weather	*It's raining* vs. *It's rainy*	Talk about the weather
	3.2 Are you busy at the moment?	Phone phrases	Present continuous	
	3.3 What are you doing these days?	Daily actions Technology problems	Present continuous	
	3.4 What do you do after school / work?		Simple present vs. Present continuous	Talk about your family
	3.5 Why are you learning English?	Adjectives (feelings)	*have to*, *want to*	
4	4.1 Do you like tennis?	Sports		Talk about sports
	4.2 Can you drive a tractor?	Abilities	*Can* ⊕ ⊖	Talk about abilities
	4.3 What languages can you speak?		*Can* ⊕ ⊖ ❓	Talk about abilities
	4.4 Are you an organized person?	Clothes & accessories	Possessive pronouns, Possessive *'s*, & *Whose*	Talk about clothes
	4.5 What shoe size are you?	Shopping expressions		
5	5.1 Is there a mall in your area?	Public places	*There is / there are* (Present) ⊕ ⊖ ❓	Describe a town
	5.2 What are your likes and dislikes?	Household chores Free-time activities	*like / love / hate / enjoy / not mind* + verb + *-ing*	Talk about likes & dislikes
	5.3 What do you like doing on vacation?	Vacation		Talk about vacation activities
	5.4 How often do you leave voice messages?	Instructions	Imperatives	
	5.5 Do you live near here?	Adjectives		Give directions

	Question syllabus	Vocabulary	Grammar	Speaking & Skills
6				
6.1	What's in your refrigerator?	Food & drink	Countable vs. uncountable nouns	Talk about food likes & dislikes
6.2	What do you eat for lunch and dinner?	Food portions	Quantifiers: *some* and *any*	Talk about a daily diet
6.3	How often do you eat chocolate?	Food & nutrition	Quantifiers: *a little, a few, a lot of*	
6.4	How many meals do you cook a week?	Recycle food portions	*How much* vs. *how many*	
6.5	What would you like for lunch?	Courses & ways to cook	*I like* vs. *I'd like*	Ordering food
7				
7.1	Do you live in a house?	Rooms & furniture	Past of *be*: *there was / there were*	
7.2	Where were you last night?	Party items	Past of *be*	Talk about parties
7.3	Where were you last New Year's Eve?	Celebrations	Prepositions of place	Talk about your town
7.4	Was your hometown different 10 years ago?	Places in a city	Past of *be* ⊕ ⊖ ?	Describe a town in the past
7.5	How about a barbecue on Sunday?			Make invitations
8				
8.1	When did you start school?	Biographies		
8.2	Did you go out last weekend?	Ordinal numbers & dates	Simple past ⊕ ⊖ Prepositions	
8.3	Where did you go on your last vacation?		Simple past ?	Pronunciation *did you* /dɪdʒə/
8.4	When do you listen to music?	Everyday activity verbs	Subject questions	Talk about past routine
8.5	Could you help me, please?		*Could*	
9				
9.1	How did you get here today?	Transportation	Recycle simple past	Talk about how you get to places
9.2	What do you do?	Jobs		Talk about jobs
9.3	Where are you going to be in 2025?	Future plans	*going to*	Talk about future plans / predictions
9.4	What are you going to do next year?	Life changes	*going to* vs. present continuous	
9.5	Would you like to be a nurse?	*borrow / lend*		Ask for permission
10				
10.1	Do you look like your mom?	The body & face Descriptions of people		Describe a person
10.2	Are you like your dad?	Adjectives (appearance & character)	Comparatives	
10.3	Who's the most generous person in your family?	Personality types	Superlatives	Express opinions about people & places
10.4	What's the best place in the world?	Geographical features		
10.5	Is your English better than a year ago?		Recycle comparatives & superlatives	

Audio script p. 54   Answer key p. 60   Phrasebank p. 64   Wordlist p. 70

1.1 Are you Canadian?

1 Put these words in the correct column.

| Africa | America | Asia | Australia | Brazil | Canada | Chile | Europe | India | Korea |

Countries	Continents

2 ▶1.1 Add *n*, *an*, or *ian* to make the adjective. Listen, check, and repeat the countries and adjectives with the correct stress.

3 Read a–e and write the country or nationality.
a I'm from Milan, in the north of ___Italy___.
b I come from a large country in Asia. The capital of my country is Delhi. I'm _____.
c My native language is Mandarin. I'm _____.
d My new phone is a Samsung. It's from _____.
e The famous Machu Picchu ruins are in my country. I'm _____.

4 ▶1.2 Listen and complete dialogues 1–5.

1 A ___Is___ Rachel Griffiths Amer_ican_?
  B No, she _isn't_. She _____ Austr_____.
2 A _____ you Chinese?
  B No, I _____. I'm Kor_____.
3 A _____ Kanul Nayyar Per_____?
  B No, he's Ind_____. He _____ from Delhi.
4 A Are they Ameri_____?
  B No, _____. They _____ Bri_____.
5 A Is Javier Bardem Mex_____?
  B No, he _____. He _____ Spa_____.

5 Check ✓ the correct sentences. Correct the mistakes in the wrong ones.
a Maradona is a̶n̶ interesting person.
b Shanghai is a fantastic city. ✓
c My brother is an horrible singer.
d You are a excellent actor.
e She is an OK writer.
f It is a special city.

6 Order the words in a–e to make sentences.
a terrible / I / a / *Star Wars* / is / think / movie / .
_____
b is / player / Luis Suárez / excellent / an / .
_____
c I / is / São Paulo / a / city /great / think / .
_____
d country / think / India / interesting / I / is / an / .
_____
e actor / Chris Pratt / cool / a / is / .
_____

7 🙂 **Make it personal** Write three ➕ and three ➖ opinions. Use these words to help you.

| an actor | a soccer player | a movie |
| a musician | a restaurant | a song | your city |

➕ *Star Wars is a great movie.*
➖ *My city isn't an excellent place.*

📶 **Connect**
Use one of your opinions in 7 to write a short tweet.

1.2 How do you spell your last name?

1 ▶ 1.3 Listen and write eight famous TV channels.
a ___
b ___
c ___
d ___
e ___
f ___
g ___
h ___

2 Cross out the word with the different vowel sound in a–g.
a a plane – a train – ~~are~~
b a shoe – go – two
c a car – a star – a name
d ten – a tree – three
e a pen – eight – twelve
f nine – wine – six
g one – go – a rose

3 ▶ 1.4 Match these pairs to the correct vowel sound group a–g in **2**. Listen to check.
- [d] she – me
- [ ] hi – five
- [ ] a guitar – a party
- [ ] no – a nose
- [ ] blue – you
- [ ] a name – Spain
- [ ] ten – yes

4 Complete the puzzle with vowels to reveal the numbers 1–10.

5 ▶ 1.5 Listen and complete dialogues 1–4. Calculate the final number.

1 A Excuse me. Can I help you?
 B Hi, these shorts and these sandals, please.
 A OK. The shorts are ___ euros and the sandals ___ euros. The total is ___ euros.
2 A Next please.
 B A train ticket to New York, please.
 A New York. That's ___ dollars.
 B Wow! Er ... OK. Here's ___.
 A Thanks. Here's your ticket and ___ dollars.
3 A How much are the donuts?
 B ___ cents each.
 A OK! Can I have ___, please?
 B That's ___ dollars. There you go. Enjoy!
4 A Valentine's Day is going to be perfect, huh?!
 B Yep! ___ red roses and a meal in a restaurant. And the roses cost ___ dollars each.
 A That's ___ dollars! That's ridiculous!

6 ▶ 1.6 Listen to check the final number.

7 😀 **Make it personal** Complete the conversation with your details.
A Hi! My name's Marty Anders, nice to meet you. I'm American and I'm from New York. I'm 14.
B Hi! Nice ___ you. My first name's ___ and my last name's ___. I'm ___. I'm from ___. I'm ___.

1.3 What's your email address?

1 ▶ 1.7 Listen and complete the form.

First name: _____
Last name: _____
Hotel address: Hotel _____ , _____ Sea Parade.
Phone: _____
Email: _____ @ _____ .com

2 ▶ 1.8 Ask questions using *what*. Follow the model.
Model: *Name.*
You: *What's your name?*
Model: *Full name.*
You: *What's your full name?*

3 Write questions.
a _____ Robert Smith
b _____ New York City
c _____ 457-3903
d _____ 4 North Avenue
e _____ smithrob@gmail.com

4 😀 Make it personal Answer questions a–e in **3** and complete a form about yourself.

5 Order the letters to spell five common objects. Then find the secret object.

O	A	P	P	T	L
1	2	3	4	5	6
L					

E	Y	K
7	8	9

W	I	N	D	C	H	A	S
10	11	12	13	14	15	16	17

S	A	G	L	E	S	S
18	19	20	21	22	23	24

E	H	N	O	P
25	26	27	28	29

1	15	25	21	4	15	16	7
_	_	_	_	_	_	_	_

6 Put these words in the correct plural box.

address backpack city country earring
glass key nationality phone sandwich

+ S

+ ES

-Y + IES

7 ▶ 1.9 Circle the correct word in dialogues 1–5.

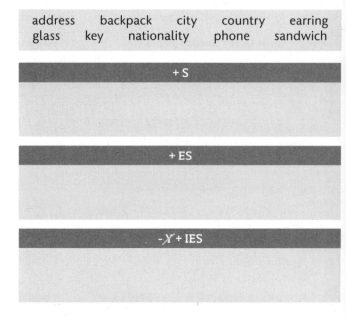

1 A **This** / **That** is my new boyfriend.
  B Oh, wow! He's cool.
2 A **This** / **That** is my family's apartment. The view is fantastic.
  B Wow! You are lucky. I can't see anything from my apartment.
3 A **This** / **These** are my new earrings. Do you like **it** / **them**?
  B Ummm. **They** / **It** are ... interesting.
4 A Excuse me. What are **these** / **those**?
  B **It** / **They** are mangos. Very fresh, very delicious. Two for a dollar.
5 A **This** / **These** roses are for you. I love you!
  B Oh, Fabio! **They** / **These** are beautiful! Thank you.

1.4 Are these your glasses?

1. Complete the photo comments with *their*, *our*, *your*, *his*, or *her*.

1. This is a photo of Tim and me on _____ vacation.
2. This is Mark with _____ horrible new sunglasses.
3. Sorry, are these _____ sunglasses?
4. Lions with _____ babies ... Fantastic!

2. **Correct the mistakes in a–f.**
   a This is Peter and her girlfriend, Sharon.
   b You are pretty. What's her name?
   c Anna loves his pretty new earrings.
   d These are ours chairs.
   e What are they're names?
   f Are these yours keys?

3. **Match phrases a–k to the answers.**

a	The American president lives there.
b	The Argentinian president lives there.
c	A famous Colombian singer.
d	World famous blue jeans.
e	A fictional black and white cartoon dog.
f	Mix red and blue to make this color.
g	The colors of the Spanish flag.
h	A little orange clown fish.
i	A red, green, or yellow fruit.
j	He lives with the dog in **e**.
k	A Black Eyed Peas song.

   Shakira
   Charlie Brown
   The White House
   Purple
   Red and yellow
   An apple
   Levi's
   "Where is the love?"
   Snoopy
   The Pink House
   Nemo

4. ▶ 1.10 Describe the objects. Follow the model.
   Model: *Car. Blue.*
   You: *It's a blue car.*
   Model: *Song. Famous.*
   You: *It's a famous song.*

   Connect
   Write short descriptions of the last three photos you took on your phone.

1.5 What's your full name?

1 Read the forms and answer a–f.

a What nationality is Lance?

b Where's Gwen from?

c What's Laurence's date of birth?

d What's the Indian woman's last name?

e How old is Priya?

f What's Lance's address?

2 ▶ 1.11 **Make it personal** Listen and answer the questions.

 Connect
*Use your phone to record your answers.
Send them to a classmate or your teacher.*

3 ▶ 1.12 Listen and choose the best response.
  a Fine, thanks. / Not really.
  b Not so good. / Not much.
  c Bye, for now. / Hi!
  d I'm well. / You're welcome.
  e I'm sorry. / Nothing much.
  f Oh, sorry. / Sure.

4 ▶ 1.12 Cover 3. Listen again and answer. Follow the model.
  Model: *How are you?*
  You: *Fine, thanks.*

Can you remember …
▶ 8 countries and nationalities? SB→p. 6
▶ 12 adjectives to give your opinion? SB→p. 7
▶ the 26 letters of the alphabet? SB→p. 8
▶ numbers 1–100? SB→p. 9
▶ 5 Wh- questions? SB→p. 10
▶ 11 everyday objects? SB→p. 11
▶ 10 colors and 6 adjectives? SB→p. 13
▶ 6 greetings? SB→p. 15

2.1 When do you get up?

1 Complete a–g with *to a*, *to the*, *to*, or *–*. For a–e, check the true sentences. Answer f and g.

a I go _____ small café in the mornings.
b We go _____ grocery store on weekends.
c I go _____ gym every day.
d I want to go _____ party tonight, but I have to go _____ work!
e I go _____ home after school.
f Do you go _____ school on Saturdays?
g Do you go _____ church?

2 ▶ 2.1 Copy the rhythm. Follow the model.

Model: *home after school.*
You: *I go home after school.*
Model: *work on Monday.*
You: *I go to work on Monday.*

3 Read the article and match the ancient gods to the days.

ORIGINS OF A NAME

The names for the days of the week in some modern languages come from the gods of Ancient Rome. For example, *Day of Venus*, the Roman goddess of love, is the modern Spanish *Viernes*. With the expansion of the Roman Empire, the Germanic and Nordic people adopted the Roman practice. They modified the system to use the corresponding gods from their culture, like *Frige*, the Nordic goddess of love. So both *Friday* and *Viernes* are the *Day of Love*!

a	The Sun	Monday
b	Mercury and *Woden*: music and poetry	Tuesday
c	Venus and *Frige*: love	Wednesday
d	The Moon	Thursday
e	Mars and *Tiw*: combat	Friday
f	Jupiter and *Thor*: Chief of Gods	Saturday
g	Saturn: Time	Sunday

4 Reread. Answer questions a–c.

a How many days have names from Nordic gods?
☐ 3   ☐ 4   ☐ 5
b Which planet gives its name to a day in English?
☐ Venus   ☐ Mercury   ☐ Saturn
c What is the most romantic day of the week?
☐ Wednesday   ☐ Thursday   ☐ Friday

5 ▶ 2.2 Listen and check the times you hear, a–e.

a ☐ 6:15   ☐ 6:45   *It's six forty-five.*
b ☐ 6:30   ☐ 7:30   _____
c ☐ 5:00   ☐ 4:00   _____
d ☐ 12:15   ☐ 12:45   _____
e ☐ 2:45   ☐ 3:15   _____

6 Write the times you don't hear in **5**.

7 Order the words in a–f to make questions.

a ? / you / do / time / go / school / to / what
_____

b ? / time / go / you / to / what / bed / do
_____

c ? / what / work / time / go / you / to / do
_____

d ? / do / home / time / what / you / get
_____

e ? / do / you / up / what / get / time
_____

f ? / to / what / you / gym / the / do / go / time
_____

8 🗣 **Make it personal** Answer questions a–f in **7**.

I go to school at 7.

📶 **Connect**

*Use your phone to record your answers.
Send them to a classmate or your teacher.*

2.2 What do you do in the mornings?

1 Match a–h to the second column to make phrases from the Student's Book.

a brush — a shower
b get — the bed
c get — breakfast
d have — dressed
e leave — my teeth
f make — home
g take — up
h wake — up

2 **Make it personal** Put the phrases in **1** in order for your morning routine.

3 ▶2.3 Read the blog post and listen. Fill in the gaps with the phrases.

| immediately | at around | for twenty minutes | at six thirty | for around |

My Morning!

I'm Alan. I'm an Olympic athlete and this is my morning routine! My alarm clock wakes me up _____ and I get out of bed _____. I exercise _____ thirty minutes **and then** I take a shower _____ and my mom prepares my breakfast. I get dressed and **after that** I have breakfast, brush my teeth, and leave the house _____ eight o'clock. **Then** I go to the gym for more exercise! I don't have time to make my bed, my mom does that for me, too. I love my mom!

4 Reread. True (T) or False (F)?
a Alan stays in bed after he wakes up.
b Alan exercises for half an hour.
c Alan takes a shower before he eats.
d Alan brushes his teeth after breakfast.
e Alan makes his bed in the morning.
f Alan leaves the house and goes to the gym.

5 **Make it personal** Write a paragraph about your morning routine using the **bold** linkers in the blog post in **3**.

6 Complete song lines A–H with *love*, *loves*, *don't love*, or *doesn't love*.

A "I _____ you like a love song, baby."
    Selena Gomez and The Scene

B "She _____ you yeah, yeah, yeah." The Beatles

C "When a man _____ a woman, he can do no wrong." Percy Sledge

D "I _____ (−) you like I loved you yesterday."
    My Chemical Romance

E "I don't ever wanna to feel like I did that day. Take me to the place I _____, take me all the way." Red Hot Chili Peppers

F "I _____ to _____, but my baby just _____ to dance." Tina Charles

G "I _____ rock 'n' roll." Joan Jett and The Blackhearts

H "As the nights go by, makes you want to die. Because your baby _____ (−) you anymore." The Carpenters

7 ▶2.4 Say the opposite. Follow the model.

Model: *I love you.*
You: *I don't love you.*

Model: *He doesn't have breakfast.*
You: *He has breakfast.*

2.3 Who do you live with?

1 ▶2.5 Listen and complete the family tree with these names.

> Alexandra   Ann   Camilla   Edward
> Peter   Richard   Sandra

2 Look at the family tree. True (T) or False (F)?
   a Edward is David's father.
   b Sandra is Camilla's aunt.
   c Edward and Alexandra have a daughter.
   d Peter and Camilla have cousins.
   e David has two brothers.
   f Peter and Camilla's grandfather is Ann.
   g Ann's husband is Richard.
   h David has a wife.
   i Camilla is Peter's sister.
   j David is an uncle.

3 Look at the family tree and complete the sentences.
   a David is Sandra's _____.
   b Ann is Richard's _____.
   c Edward is Peter and Camilla's _____.
   d Sandra is Edward's _____.
   e Richard is Camilla's _____.
   f Peter is Alexandra's _____.
   g Camilla is Sandra's _____.
   h Peter is Ann and Richard's _____.

4 Order the words in a–e to make questions.
   a your / what / full / name / is / ? /
   _____
   b from / you / where / are / ?
   _____
   c live / where / you / do / ?
   _____
   d city / you / like / this / do / ?
   _____
   e a / do / have / you / family / big / ?
   _____

5 **Make it personal** Answer the questions in 4.

6 Write questions for these answers a–e.
   a _____
      Her name is Mariana.
   b _____
      My sister lives in Bogotá.
   c _____
      Yes. She loves Bogotá.
   d _____
      That old man is my grandfather.
   e _____
      No, he isn't Chinese. He's Japanese.

2.4 When do you check your phone?

1 Read the information in the chart and complete the sentences with these words.

always   never   occasionally   often   sometimes

	Pedro	Ana	Luca	Sara	Jacob
check phone at breakfast	✓✓✓	✓✓✓✓	✓✓	✓	✓✓✓
text friends at school	✓	✓✓✓✓	✓✓	✓✓✓	✓
email homework to teacher	✓✓	✗	✓✓✓	✗	✓
take phone to the gym	✗	✓✓	✓	✓✓✓	✓✓✓✓
play games on phone	✓✓✓✓	✗	✓✓✓✓	✓✓	✓✓✓
watch movies on computer	✓	✓✓✓	✓✓	✓✓	✗
leave phone at home	✗	✗	✗	✓	✓✓

a Pedro ___always___ plays games on his phone.
b Sara _____ takes her phone to the gym.
c Jacob _____ emails his homework to his teacher.
d Luca and Sara _____ watch movies on the computer.
e Ana _____ texts her friends at school.
f Jacob _____ checks his phone at breakfast.
g Pedro, Ana, and Luca _____ leave their phones at home.

2 Use the information in the chart to write five different sentences about the teenagers.

a _____
b _____
c _____
d _____
e _____

3 🎤 **Make it personal** Write sentences about how often you do these things.

text your friends at school _____
call your grandparents _____
go to the gym _____
play games on your phone _____

📶 Connect

Use your questions to interview a classmate. Record their answers on your phone.

2.5 How do you celebrate your birthday?

1 Add the missing word to questions a–g.
   a How old are you?
   b Where you live?
   c you have a boyfriend / girlfriend?
   d What time you go to bed on weekdays?
   e Do you any brothers or sisters?
   f Do use the Internet?
   g What you do on the weekend?

2 **Make it personal** Write your personal answers to a–g in **1**.

3 Order these words to make follow-up questions.
   1 name / ? / is / what / his / her

   2 your / is / when / ? / birthday

   3 use / often / ? / you / do / it / how

   4 do / many / sleep / ? / you / how / hours

   5 weekdays / do / on / ? / you / what / do

   6 a / is / cool / ? / city / it

   7 old / are / how / they / ?

4 Match follow-up questions 1–7 in **3** to a–g in **1**.

5 Complete the adverbs with *a*, *e*, *o*, or *u* and number them in order of frequency, 1–6.
   ☐ __lw__ys
   ☐ n__v__r
   ☐ __cc__si__n__lly
   ☐ __ft__n
   ☐ s__m__tim__s
   ☐ __s__ __lly

6 **Make it personal** Use the adverbs in **5** to make sentences a–i true for you.
   a I go to parties. *I sometimes go to parties.*
   b I go out on the weekend.
   c I go to a party for New Year's Eve.
   d I play soccer.
   e My mom talks on the phone when she drives.
   f My father prepares meals.
   g I study English at home.
   h I give my father a gift on Father's Day.
   i I get up early on the weekend.

7 ◯ 2.6 Look at photos 1–6. What can you say in each situation? Listen to check.
   a H_____ b_____!
   b H_____ N_____ Y_____!
   c Have a g_____ t_____!
   d M_____ C_____!
   e C_____!
   f Enjoy y_____ m_____!

Can you remember ...
- 8 *go* phrases with places around town? SB→p.18
- the days of the week? SB→p.18
- how to tell the time? SB→p.19
- 10 verbs for your morning routine? SB→p.20
- words for family? SB→p.22
- how to ask yes / no questions? SB→p.23
- 6 verbs for your cell phone? SB→p.25
- 6 frequency adverbs? SB→p.25
- 6 phrases for special occasions? SB→p.27

3.1 What's the weather like?

1 Match song lines a–f to pictures 1–6. Complete the song line with a weather word.

Some Famous Weather Songs

a The ___fog___ is so thick, I can't see my hands. *The Wallflowers*

b I'm singing in the _____. What a glorious feeling, I'm happy again. *Gene Kelly*

c The answer, my friend, is blowing in the _____. *Bob Dylan*

d Hey! You! Get off of my _____. Don't hang around 'cause two is a crowd. *Rolling Stones*

e Here comes the _____, and I say it's alright. *The Beatles*

f But as long as you love me so, let it _____, let it _____, let it _____. *Dean Martin*

2 ▶3.1 Make sentences about the weather. Follow the model.

Model: *Wow! Look at the sun.*
You: *Yeah, it is really sunny today.*

3 🅐 **Make it personal** Cross out one extra word in each question. Then, answer a–e.
a What's it the weather like today?
b Is it hot in out?
c What does is the weather usually like in your city?
d How is the weather in these days?
e Is it snowy in July in the your country?

4 ▶3.2 Listen and match these answers to the questions in **3**.
☐ It's usually very windy, but today it's calm.
☐ Yes, in some places. You need a warm jacket.
☐ It's really nice. Very warm and sunny, I love it.
☐ It's cold and rainy. Yuck.
☐ Yes, it is. It's 40 degrees. I hate it.

5 Choose the correct form.
a The weather in my city is really crazy. Sometimes it's **sun / sunny** but **cold / clouds** in the morning, but in the afternoon it's **warm / warming** and **rain / rainy**.
b I don't like **rain / rainy** days. I love **hot / hotty**, **sun / sunny** weather.
c I like to stay home and watch TV when it's **snow / snowing**. It's too **cold / cool** to be outdoors.
d My best friend prefers to go to the beach when it's **cloud / cloudy**. I think she's afraid of the **sun / sunny**.
e London is famous for its **fog / foggy**, but, in my opinion, it's more probable for a tourist to see **fog / foggy** days in San Francisco than in London.

14

3.2 Are you busy at the moment?

1 Maya is writing to her friend in Finland. Use the map to cross out the wrong answer in the first paragraph. Complete the months in the other paragraphs.

From: Maya
To: Heidi
Subject: My city!

Hi Heidi,

My name is Maya and I'm from Trinidad and Tobago, two **islands** / **mountains** in the **Mediterranean** / **the Caribbean**. Port-of-Spain, is **an island** / **the capital** and it's located in the **southeast** / **northwest** of Trinidad, the **big** / **small** island. I live there!

There are only two seasons here. The dry season starts in J__u__r__ and ends in J__n__ and the wet season goes from J__l__ to D__c____b__r. If you like hot weather and nice beaches, this is the perfect place for a vacation. It's never cold here. The temperatures in the rainy season are similar to the temperatures when it's sunny and dry. The only bad thing about our weather is the wind. Sometimes, it's very strong!

Anyway, the best time to visit is during Carnival, in F__b__u____y or M_____h! Our Carnival is famous. We dance to calypso or soca, our local music. You have to see it. It's just wonderful!

Email me, please. I want to know more about you and your city.

Maya

---

2 Reread the email. True (T) or False (F)?
a Maya lives in the Caribbean.
b Port-of-Spain is only the capital of Trinidad.
c Trinidad is to the south of Tobago.
d There is no winter in Maya's country.
e Winds are cold in Trinidad and Tobago.
f Carnival is in the rainy season.

3 Complete the reply with the present continuous form of the verbs in parentheses.

From: Heidi
To: Maya
Subject: Re: My city!

Hi Maya,
I live in Kokkola, a small town in Finland. Winter _____ (**start**) here and it's very cold. Daytime _____ (**get**) shorter and nights _____ (**become**) longer. Right now my brother _____ (**do**) his homework and my mom _____ (**buy**) groceries at the store.
I _____ (**write**) to you on his laptop, so I don't have a lot of time. Talk to you later, OK?
Best,
Heidi

---

4 ▶3.3 Choose the correct phone phrases to complete dialogues 1–4. There are two extra phrases. Listen to check.

No problem.	I can't hear you.
Are you busy?	Don't worry.
The line's busy.	My battery's dying.
Call you later.	Sorry, wrong number.

1 A _____?
  B Sorry, yes. I'm at work.
  A OK, _____.
2 A Hi. Do you want to meet me at 8?
  B Can you repeat that? Sorry? _____.
  A _____. I said, "Do you want to meet me at 8?"
3 A Hello?
  B Is this Hannah?
  A Uh, no.
  B _____.
4 A Call Mike now.
  B I am calling him. _____.

3.3 What are you doing these days?

1 Match dialogues 1–6 to photos a–f.

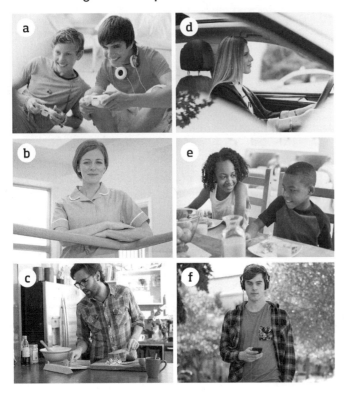

1. A Is Dad making lunch? I'm hungry.
   B Yes, he his.
2. A Where's Maria?
   B She's driving to see her grandmother in hospital.
3. A Is that Jordan walking across the street?
   B Yes, and he's listening to music on his phone again.
4. A What are they doing now?
   B They're playing video games.
5. A Where's your sister working these days?
   B She's a nurse in our local hospital.
6. A Hurry up! What are you doing?
   B We're eating our breakfast.

2 Order the words to make questions. Then write answers in the present continuous using the words in parentheses.

a your / sleeping / is / mom ?
   _No,_ _____ (working)
b doing / you / the kitchen / are / in / what ?
   _____ (make cookies)
c he / where / these days / is / living ?
   _____ (Mexico City)
d with / is / dancing / who / brother / your ?
   _____ (his girlfriend)
e playing / are / tennis / they ?
   _____ (basketball)
f what / you / drinking / now / are ?
   _____ (a cup of coffee)

3 ▶3.4 Make sentences about the photos. Follow the model.

Model: *Photo 1. What's she doing?*
You: *She's reading the newspaper.*

4 Match what each speaker says to one of these problems.

consumerism   identity theft   Internet addiction
        isolation   violence

a *My little brother is always sitting in his room playing video games and doesn't have any friends.*
   _____

b *I think our city is very bad now. My grandparents won't go out at night because of all the fighting.*
   _____

c *My sisters are always at the shopping mall buying new things. I don't understand it – why do they want so many clothes and shoes?*
   _____

d *I don't like using my computer for banking. I don't want people to take my personal information and get my money.*
   _____

e *Some people are on their computers for 20 hours a day. They are playing games, shopping, or reading the news.*
   _____

3.4 What do you do after school / work?

1 Answer the questions about these celebrities.
Who is this?
What does he / she do?
What is he / she doing now?

actor   athlete   activist   singer

a Usain Bolt
This is Usain Bolt.
He _____
Now he _____

b Emma Watson

c Drake

d Malala Yousafzai

2 🎤 **Make it personal** Write about your own family.
My father is _____
He usually _____
At the moment he _____

3 ▶ 3.5 Complete dialogues 1–4. Choose the correct verb form. Listen to check.

1 A Hi! What **do you do / are you doing** here?
   B I'm just **drinking a coffee / drink a coffee** and **relax / relaxing** on my break.
   A I see. But, what **do you do / are you doing**?
   B I'm a teacher. I always **having a coffee / have a coffee** on my break.

2 A Excuse me. What is that? I mean, what kind of motorcycle **do you ride / are you riding**?
   B Today I **ride / am riding** a scooter, but I have two motorcycles. I usually **am riding / ride** my big Harley.
   A OK, thanks.

3 A So, what **are you reading / do you read**?
   B Oh, it's a story about Shakira and Piqué. They are …
   A No, I mean … What are you reading? You **aren't / don't** usually **reading / read** *Hello!*.
   B Oh! No, you're right. I usually **read / am reading** *The New Yorker*, but I … er … I **am liking / like** the pictures in this kind of magazine.

4 A Mom! Lucy and her friends **are watching / watch** a movie!
   B Yes, that's right. They **watch / are watching** *Pitch Perfect*.
   A But, Mom, it's 6 o'clock. I always **am watching / watch** *Sunny Street* at 6.
   B Well, you can miss one day. The story is always the same, anyway.

4 Complete with the present continuous or simple present of the verbs in parentheses.

········· **Are BASE jumpers crazy?** ·········

Jack Agnello and Logan Reed _____ (**be**) BASE jumpers. They _____ (**jump**) from buildings, antennas, bridges, and mountains and they _____ (**use**) parachutes to land safely. At the moment, they _____ (**plan**) their next jump. They _____ (**want**) to jump from a bridge in West Virginia, but they _____ (**need**) to get permission to do it, so Logan _____ (**fill**) out a form at the moment while Jack _____ (**check**) the West Virginia BASE website to get more information. They are very excited about it!

3.5 Why are you learning English?

1 Complete these forum replies with *have to* or *want to*.

Q Why learn English?

ilmalearning
I _____ do my master's in the U.S., so I need to learn English quickly. I _____ get a qualification, too!

melissasoares
For pleasure. I just love languages. Oh, and for fun, too, because I _____ understand movies and songs in English.

businessman23
For professional reasons. I _____ learn for my current job. I need to study hard now because I _____ write emails in English every day. It's difficult.

alexparentes
I _____ communicate with my friends in the UK. I play online games with them and we all _____ speak in English. It's the language everyone knows.

2 ▶3.6 Listen to the interview and write the letter of activities, a–f, according to what you hear.
 a get up early
 b be at the station at 6:30
 c work on weekends
 d prepare the evening presentation
 e change jobs
 f get married and have kids

	want to		have to	
	+	–	+	–
Taylor				
Josh and Isobel				
Serena				

3 ▶3.6 Listen again and answer the questions.
 a What does Taylor do?
 b What does Serena do?
 c What do Josh and Isobel do?
 d What does Serena want to be in the future?

4 🔵 **Make it personal** Write one or two sentences about why you are learning English. Use *want to* and *have to*.

5 ▶3.7 Sarah is taking care of her son, Philip. Listen to check the symptoms.

| cold | hot | hungry | thirsty | tired |

6 Order the words in a–g to make offers for Philip. Which ones are good ideas?
 a drink / you / ? / a / do / want / cold
 b hot / you / a / would / drink / ? / like
 c you / ? / do / a / sweater / want
 d at / would / to / today / ? / you / home / like / stay
 e out / ? / to / want / you / go / do
 f ? / sandwich / a / would / like / you
 g to / you / go / do / ? / to / want / hospital

Can you remember ...
▶ 6 weather words?   SB→p. 32
▶ 4 temperature words?   SB→p. 32
▶ 6 activities?   SB→p. 34
▶ the 12 months?   SB→p. 35
▶ 6 seasons?   SB→p. 35
▶ 5 more activities?   SB→p. 38
▶ 2 ways of offering?   SB→p. 41

4.1 Do you like tennis?

1 Complete a–f with the sports for each ball. Then complete g and h to find two more sports.

a
b
c
d
e
f
g
h

2 Circle the sport that is different and match it to the reason.
a basketball, golf, soccer, rugby
b golf, tennis, baseball, volleyball
c cycling, swimming, surfing, windsurfing
d soccer, swimming, cycling, running
e skateboarding, golf, skiing, football

☐ You don't do it in water.
☐ You have to score points.
☐ You use your hands to hit the ball.
☐ You can only do it in winter.
☐ It isn't a team game.

3 ▶ 4.1 Listen to parents, Rob and Claire, talking about their children's sports. Complete the schedule with the sports. There are extra sports.

ballet   baseball   basketball   soccer   swimming   tennis   volleyball

	Chloe	Randy
Monday		soccer
Tuesday		
Wednesday		
Thursday		
Friday		
Saturday		
Sunday		

4 ▶ 4.1 Listen again and answer the questions.
a Who is practicing sports today?
b What time does Chloe's swimming practice start?
c What time does it finish?
d Who has to take the children to volleyball practice?

5 ▶ 4.2 **Make it personal** Listen and say *I love / like / don't like / hate* + the sports. Follow the model.
Model: *baseball*
You: *I like baseball. / I don't like baseball.*

4.2 Can you drive a tractor?

1 Complete the groups with these words.

| a bus | a car | Chinese | Indian food | the drums | soccer |
| French | Korean | the piano | pasta | a special meal | a tractor |

- **play**: the violin, ...
- **drive**: a truck, ...
- **speak**: English, ...
- **cook**: Japanese food, ...

2 Read the interview. Match questions a–d to the answers.

Interview with soccer player Patrice Garnier

a What are your favorite sports to watch and to play?
b Can you play a musical instrument?
c Can you cook well?
d What languages can you speak?

☐ I have a restaurant in Milan, it serves Japanese food, but, no, I can't cook very well. My partner, Lisa, does the cooking. She can cook anything, she's fantastic.

☐ Of course I love soccer, to play and to watch. It really is a beautiful game. But I also like swimming and tennis, they are good for training, too. I think I can play tennis well.

☐ I really like learning other languages, and they're useful for my profession. I'm from France, so my native language is French. I can also speak English, Spanish, and Italian.

☐ I can play the guitar, and I can sing. I have some songs on an Italian compilation album, with a collection of other "artists"! I sing a Bob Marley song, "Redemption Song," and an old soul song, "Sitting on the Dock of the Bay," by Otis Redding.

3 Reread. Answer questions a–d.
a Why does Patrice like tennis and swimming?
b Does Patrice sing original songs?
c Who prepares the food in Patrice's restaurant?
d How many languages can he speak?
e What two reasons does he give for learning languages?
f Why does he like watching soccer?

4 🔊 **Make it personal** Complete the box with a ✓ or ✗. Then write true sentences about you.

Activities	Can / Can't?
Play soccer	
Swim	
Cook a meal	
Ride a bicycle	
Drive a car	
Speak French	

I can _____
I can't _____

4.3 What languages can you speak?

1 Complete these song lines with **can** or **can't**. Do you know these songs?

a "I know I _____, I know I _____, be what I wanna be." **Nas**
b "Please _____ you, make this work for me?" **Sam Smith**
c "I _____ make you love me when you don't." **Adele**
d "You _____ remember my name." **Ed Sheeran**
e "I _____ live, if living is without you. I _____ give, I _____ give any more." **Mariah Carey**
f "_____ remember to forget you." **Shakira**
g "I _____ see you're sad, even when you smile, even when you laugh." **Eminem**
h "_____ you feel the love tonight?" **Elton John**

2 Write questions and answers about the people in the photos.

Jack

Chloe

Maria

a play / piano (✓)
   Can Jack play the piano?
   Yes, he can.

b cook? (✗)

c drive / car ? (✓)

Kyle

Sam

Amy

d play / violin? (✗)

e swim ? (✓)

f ski ? (✗)

3 ⏵4.3 Ben can do everything well, but his brother Lance can't do anything very well! Make sentences about them. Follow the model.

Model: *Ben, bike*
You: *Ben can ride a bike very well.*
Model: *Lance, Japanese*
You: *Lance can't speak Japanese very well.*

4 🅐 Make it personal Make true sentences with **can** or **can't**. Add **very well**, or **at all** when necessary.

a I _____ use Google _____.
b I _____ understand directions _____.
c I _____ cook _____.
d I _____ remember names _____.
e I _____ use simple tools _____.
f I _____ speak two languages _____.
g I _____ bargain _____.
h I _____ make a good first impression.

4.4 Are you an organized person?

1 Look at the photo and answer questions a–i.
  a What's the young boy wearing?
  b How many people are wearing ties?
  c Are all of the people wearing shoes?
  d Are all of the women wearing belts?
  e Which person has a suit?
  f Who's wearing a skirt?
  g Are all of the men wearing shirts?
  h How many people are wearing shorts?
  i How many people are wearing a dress?

2 Write a description of one of these people and exchange it with a friend. Can you guess which person it is?

3 Order the clothes items to complete tweets a–e.

a I am at the shopping mall. Need to buy a new ____dress____ (sdrse) and new _____ (sseoh) for a party tonight.

b Cute _____ (asasdln) but too expensive at my fave store. Maybe _____ (oostb)?

c _____ (sdrse) I like is too small ☹.

d Checking a _____ (uoesbl) and a _____ (kitrs) now. Finally!

e Really happy with this green _____ (hrtis) and white skirt. Only 75 too! ☺

4 Read the tweets and answer a–e.
  a What does she initially want to buy?
  b What do you think *fave* probably means?
  c What does she buy at the end?
  d How much do the clothes cost?
  e Do you know anyone like Carol?

5 Read the blog and complete it with:

's	hers	his	mine	ours
theirs	whose	yours		

Which girl doesn't have a shoe collection? I know I do. _____ is 10 pairs, including shoes, boots, and sandals. How about _____? But _____ are small compared to some celebrities. My collection fills a closet, _____ fill entire rooms!

Khloe Kardashian has a huge closet. In fact it's the same size as two bedrooms! Khloe _____ closet is full of designer clothes, shoes, and bags and it is very well organized. All the shoes are organized by colors!

Poor Kendall Jenner says _____ is too small for all her clothes and it is very messy, so every two months she gives a lot of her unworn shoes and clothes to thrift stores. Then she can buy more designer goods to put back in the closet!

Even male celebrities like Mark Wahlberg have GIGANTIC shoe collections. _____ collection of 137 pairs of sneakers cost $100,000!

These celebrities have so many shoes I wonder if they ever ask "_____ shoes are these?"

6 ▶ 4.4 Ask questions using *whose*. Follow the model.
Model: *socks*
You: *Whose socks are these?*
Model: *sweater*
You: *Whose sweater is this?*

7 **Make it personal** Answer these questions about you.
  a How many pairs of shoes do you have?
  b How many pairs of jeans do you have?
  c What do you usually wear to work?
  d What do you wear to a wedding?

4.5 What shoe size are you?

1 Match a–e to the photos.
 a credit card
 b the fitting rooms
 c contactless
 d a receipt
 e the store window

2 ▶4.5 Order these words to make a dialogue. Complete with words from **1**.

Salesclerk you / can / ? / hi / help / I / ,
Jason   in / can / I / _____ / shorts / ? / hello / on / those / , / try
Salesclerk are / here / , / you / sure / .
            there / _____ / over / are / .
Jason   great / are / they / !
            I / ? / _____ / pay / by / can
Salesclerk course / of / .
            it / is / _____ / ?
Jason   is / Yes / it / .
            ? / have / _____ / please / , / can / I

3 ▶4.6 Imagine you are at a store. The salesclerk shows you an item of clothing. Respond as in the examples. Follow the model.

Model: *brown coat*
You: *Can I try that brown coat on?*
Model: *blue jeans*
You: *Can I try those blue jeans on?*

4 ▶4.7 Listen to Katie and her boyfriend, Brian, in a shopping mall. Answer a–e.
 a Does Brian like shopping?
  ☐ Yes, he does.
  ☐ No, he doesn't.
  ☐ He thinks it's OK.
 b What kind of store are they in?
  ☐ A sports store.
  ☐ A clothes store.
  ☐ A shoe store.
 c What size jeans does Brian need?
  ☐ S
  ☐ M
  ☐ L
 d How much are the shorts?
  ☐ $16
  ☐ $46
  ☐ $60
 e What does Katie buy in the end?
  ☐ Nothing.
  ☐ A blouse.
  ☐ A pair of shorts.

5 ▶4.8 Imagine you are shopping with Katie. Respond to the questions. Follow the model.

Model: *What do you think of these boots?*
You: *I like them. They look great.*
Model: *What do you think of this blouse?*
You: *I like it. It looks great.*

6 🔵 Make it personal Tell your partner about the clothes and shoes you like wearing.

Connect
*Use the dialogue in **2** to practice a similar one with your partner. Record your dialogue and send it to your teacher.*

Can you remember ...
▶ 7 sports? SB→p. 44
▶ 10 activities? SB→p. 46
▶ 10 abilities? SB→p. 49
▶ 4 professions? SB→p. 49
▶ 16 clothes items? SB→p. 50
▶ 6 possessive pronouns? SB→p. 51
▶ 4 clothes sizes? SB→p. 53
▶ the place where you try on clothes? SB→p. 53

5

5.1 Is there a mall in your area?

1 Complete the puzzle with places around town.

Across
1 You watch movies in a _____.
3 The Nile is a very long _____.
8 You buy books at a _____.
9 You can dance at a _____.

Down
2 You pay to swim in a _____.
3 Cars or horses compete at a _____.
4 You can have a picnic in a _____.
5 There are hundreds of stores at a _____.
6 You stay in a _____ when you go on vacation.
7 You take books from a _____ but only for a week or two.

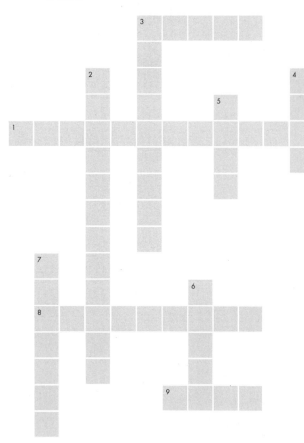

2 ▶5.1 Listen, mark the stress and the number of syllables in words a–h.

E.g.: Sy·lla·ble. ●○○

a bar
b club
c hotel
d museum
e park
f restaurant
g stadium
h theater

3 🎧 Make it personal Use the words in **1** and **2** to make true sentences for you.
a There's a fantastic _____ in my town.
b I think a _____ is an interesting place.
c There isn't a _____ near my house.
d There's a _____ near my house.
e There's more than one _____ in my town.
f My favorite _____ is called _____.

4 🎧 Make it personal Order the words to make sentences. Are they true for your town?
a 's / downtown / museum / a / there / .
b no / are / theaters / movie / here / there / .
c big / there / any / parks / aren't / .
d some / good / restaurants / are / there / .
e a / bookstore / 's / fantastic / there / .
f there / small / are / rivers / two / .

5 Complete the song lines with **there is**, (or **there's**) **there are**, **is there**, or **are there**.

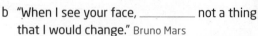

a "Imagine _____ no heaven."
  John Lennon
b "When I see your face, _____ not a thing that I would change." Bruno Mars
c "_____ nothin' you can't do now you're in New York." Alicia Keys
d "_____ many things that I would like to say to you, but I don't know how." Oasis
e "_____ a lady who's sure all that glitters is gold, and she's buying a stairway to heaven."
  Led Zeppelin
f "_____ anybody going to listen to my story?"
  The Beatles
g "_____ a chance for me?" Frank Sinatra
h "And though _____ times when I hate you"
  Beyoncé
i "_____ any more real cowboys?" Neil Young

📶 **Connect**

Try to find these songs online. What's your favorite one?

5.2 What are your likes and dislikes?

1 ▶5.2 Guess which of the phrases below complete crazy statistics a–h. Listen to check.

cleaning the house   cooking   eating out   exercising
going out   playing video games   shopping   watching TV

What a life!
Where does all our time go? Look at these crazy statistics.

a American men spend about 3 hours a week _____.
b On average, French people spend 32 minutes a day _____.
c Americans spend approximately 50 minutes a day _____.
d 58% of Americans like _____ once a week.
e On average, American men spend 13.3 hours a week _____.
f Only 53% of British teenagers like _____ on weekends.
g Americans spend about 98 hours a month _____.
h American teens spend about 1 hour a day _____.

2 ▶5.3 Express your emotions! Follow the model.

Model: *cleaning the house. Sad!*
You: *I hate cleaning the house!*
Model: *watching TV. OK.*
You: *I don't mind watching TV.*
Model: *eating out. Happy!*
You: *I love eating out.*

3 ▶5.4 Listen to Leo and Becky talking about the statistics in **1**. Which activity do they both like?

4 Complete the labels with these verbs and match them to photos a–f.

Clean   Do   Play   Tidy   Wash   Watch

☐ _____ the laundry.
☐ _____ my bedroom.
☐ _____ a movie.
☐ _____ the dishes.
☐ _____ video games.
☐ _____ the bathroom.

5 Read the extract and answer a and b.
a Where is the extract from?
☐ A book.
☐ A newspaper.
☐ A poster.
b The extract is …
☐ selling a product.
☐ for fun.
☐ giving information.

6 ▶5.5 Listen and complete a–h with the correct form of the verbs.

TV! week | **Modern Families. 8:45 p.m. Channel 5**
Recent statistics show that parents do most of the housework, around 9 hours a week compared to teenagers' 4.9 hours. In this episode, the team is talking to Celia Monroe, 49, and her son, Angelo, 15, about how this affects their lives and their free time.

a Angelo _____ doing his laundry.
b Angelo absolutely _____ washing the dishes.

hate (x2)   have   like (x2)   love (x2)
mind (x2)   clean

c He never _____ his room.
d He _____ playing video games and watching movies.
e Celia _____ doing the chores.
f Celia _____ washing the dishes.
g She _____ cleaning the bathroom.
h She _____ time for free time activities.
i She _____ to swim when she can.
j She _____ to read novels.

Connect
Use your phone to record yourself talking about your likes and dislikes.

5.3 What do you like doing on vacation?

1 Read the article about the Galápagos islands and match the highlighted words to the photos.

There are over 50 islands in the Galápagos archipelago, and there are many ways to explore them. Snorkeling. Biking. Walking. Kayaking. Just select the option for you, or try all of them in our exclusive vacation package!
What to do: There are thousands of unique birds and animals here, and you can come face-to-face with wonderful wildlife. Swim with penguins on Bartolomé island. Go snorkeling on Floreana and see the turtles or the pink flamingoes in the lagoons. See sea lions on the white sand beaches of San Cristóbal, or travel to the quiet forests of the island to find the giant tortoises.

2 ▶5.6 Reread and answer a–d. Listen to check.
  a What three activities can you do in the sea?
  b Do you have to choose **one** way to explore the islands?
  c Do tortoises live in the sea?
  d Find five examples of wildlife.

3 What do Katy, Sara, and Tom like doing on vacation? Choose the best three activities for each person.

snorkeling   sightseeing   sunbathing   camping   kayaking   swimming   reading novels
    visiting museums   eating out

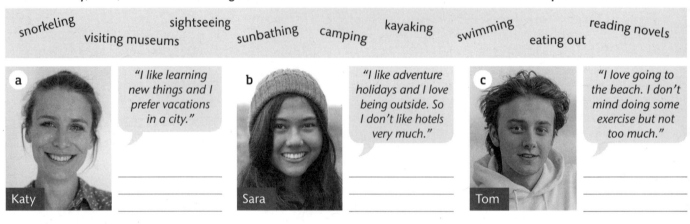

a Katy: "I like learning new things and I prefer vacations in a city."

b Sara: "I like adventure holidays and I love being outside. So I don't like hotels very much."

c Tom: "I love going to the beach. I don't mind doing some exercise but not too much."

4 **Make it personal** Complete the puzzle with vacation activities. For example, ☠ = N. Check the ones that you like doing.

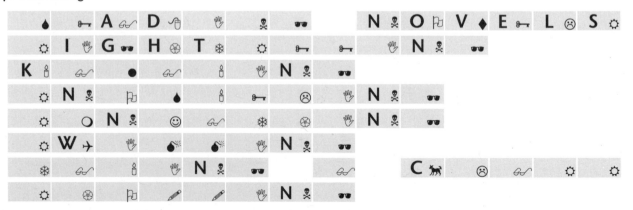

5.4 How often do you leave voice messages?

1 ▶5.7 Complete the blog with the correct form of these words. Listen to check.

check   close   feed   give   let   open   pick   put   take (x2)   wash   water

Beth's Blog

Hi everyone! Here I am in the beautiful city of Bath. I've got a new job for the summer – I'm a house sitter. The family are in New York on holiday and I'm _____ care of their house, garden, two dogs, one cat, and lots of fish!

It's a big house with a garden and I have a list of chores I have to do every day. Most of them are fun and I don't mind doing them, but I don't like _____ the plants. They have lots and lots of plants!!

It's very hot here this summer, so every morning I _____ the windows and doors and _____ the cat out. He usually sleeps under a tree all day. Then I _____ the dogs, Toby and Freddie, and _____ the fish some food – they have 8 beautiful fish. I _____ there is some clean water for the cat, and after breakfast I _____ the dogs for a long walk. They love going to the park and swimming in the lake there.

When I get home, I _____ up the mail and _____ it on the table in the kitchen. I spend most of the day reading or sunbathing in the garden. Sometimes I go sightseeing in Bath. It's brilliant!

In the evening I _____ the windows, _____ the dishes, and go to bed. I don't get paid for this job, but I love being a house sitter.

2 Read the blog again and answer a–c.
 a Where is Beth living now?
 b What does the cat like doing?
 c How much money does Beth get every week?

3 ▶5.8 Listen to four phone messages. Check ✓ (do) or cross ✗ (don't do) the activities.
 a Water the plants.   Feed the cat.   Close the windows.
 b Cook dinner.   Prepare a salad.   Wash the dishes.
 c Take the dog for a walk. Feed the dog.   Feed the cat.
 d Buy some herbal tea.   Clean the house today.   Go to the grocery store.

4 Complete instructions a–e.

a _____ the windows in the morning and close _____ again at _____. Thanks.

b Remember to phone Mom and sing _____ "Happy Birthday." XXX

c After dinner, _____ forget to wash the _____ and dry _____!!!

d Your brother wants you to call _____ after 7 p.m.

e Buy some coffee and leave _____ on the kitchen table. Thanks.

5.5 Do you live near here?

1 ▶5.9 Complete a–e with these adjectives. Listen to check.

| boring | cheap | messy | near | safe |

a It's not dangerous to swim here—it's _____. Look! There are a lot of people swimming.
b What do you mean it's expensive? It's only $80. That's very _____ for a tablet.
c My office is very tidy. I hate _____ rooms.
d I like history, it's really interesting. But I always sleep in my math class. It's so _____.
e I live quite far from downtown, but there's a good shopping mall _____ my house.

2 Read this magazine article. True (T) or False (F)?

Camping – but not as you know it!

Do you think that camping equals cold, rain, insects in your clothes, and no showers? Do you think that camping is cheap but messy? Not anymore. "Glamping" is the new craze in vacations—you stay in a tent, but it's a five-star tent. Camping with glamour! If you want to go glamping here are some tips:

- Search the Internet for a good price. It can be expensive!
- Remember to take stylish but warm clothes. You want to look good, not blue with cold!
- Recharge your phone before you go. There isn't always electricity on campgrounds, even glamorous ones!
- Take an umbrella. You can't change the weather and you don't want your hair to get wet!

a Camping is always messy.
b "Glamping" is a recent idea.
c Glamping usually costs more than camping.
d You can always watch TV when glamping.

3 Match new words 1–4 to definitions a–d.

1 a gray**cation**
2 info**tain**ment
3 **net**iquette
4 a **scree**nager

a being polite on the Internet
b a young person that watches TV, plays video games and uses the Internet all the time
c a TV show that mixes facts with fun
d staying with your grandparents to save money

4 ▶5.10 Listen and mark these buildings on the map.

| bookstore | club | gym |
| ID English | museum | |

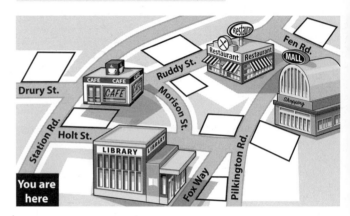

5 ▶5.11 Ask for directions. Follow the model.
Model: *Do you know. Library?*
You: *Do you know where the library is?*
Model: *Mall. Near here?*
You: *Is there a mall near here?*

6 ▶5.12 Answer the questions. Follow the model.
Model: *Is there a café near here?*
You: *Yeah, there's one on Station Road.*

7 **Make it personal** Write directions from school to your favorite place in your city.

1. *Leave school and turn ...*

Can you remember ...

- 16 places around town? SB→p. 58
- how to describe your town? SB→p. 59
- 10 things you do in your free time? SB→p. 60
- 4 verbs to talk about what you prefer to do? SB→p. 60
- 14 vacation activities? SB→p. 62
- how to leave a message telling someone what to do? SB→p. 64
- 9 adjectives? SB→p. 66
- 2 new English words for vacations? SB→p. 66
- how to ask for directions? SB→p. 67

6.1 What's in your refrigerator?

1 Write food items a–j and reveal the mystery sentence.

a ▢▢▢▢▢▢▢▢▢
   35 23 32   7 2

b ▢▢▢▢
   33 39

c ▢▢▢▢▢
   28 5 30 1

d ▢▢▢▢▢
   38 8 34 36

e ▢▢▢
   11 37

f ▢▢▢▢▢
   27 18 21 6 9

g ▢▢▢▢
   3 14 25 19

h ▢▢▢▢▢▢
   29 17 4 12 20 31

i ▢▢▢▢
   13 26   22

j ▢▢▢▢
   16 24 10 15

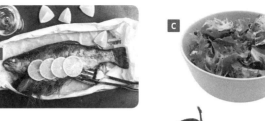

W		W													Y				
1		2	3	4	5	6	7	8	9	10	11	12	13	14	15	16	17	18	19 20

		D		B														
21	22	23	24	25	26	27	28	29	30	31	32	33	34	35	36	37	38	39

2 ▶ 6.1 Listen to the dialogue and write the shopping list.

3 ▶ 6.1 Listen again and complete a–e.
  a They need tea because Hannah used _____ last night.
  b They are going to eat _____ for _____.
  c The mother is going to cook the _____ with _____ and _____.
  d The mother wants some _____ because she likes to eat them for _____.
  e Hannah wants some _____.

4 🎧 **Make it personal** Which of the food in exercise **1** do you like and which do you not like?
  I like _____ and I like _____, but I don't like _____.

5 Classify the food items in the pictures below as countable or uncountable.

Countable	Uncountable

6.2 What do you eat for lunch and dinner?

1 Match photos a–i to these words.

☐ a bottle ☐ a can ☐ a glass ☐ a slice
☐ a bowl ☐ a cup ☐ a piece

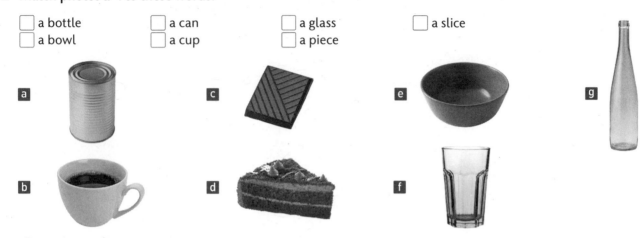

2 ▶ 6.2 Complete with *some*, *any*, or *a(n)*. Listen to check.

Gina Hi, Mona. Would you like _____ cookies?
Mona No, thanks, Gina. I can't eat _____ cookies today.
Gina Why not? Are you on _____ diet?
Mona No, I'm not, but I have _____ test today and I can't eat _____ sugar or I get very nervous.
Gina Really?
Mona Yes. Last time I had a test I ate _____ chocolate before and my heart went crazy! And there was _____ information that I was sure that I knew but couldn't remember. So, I don't eat _____ sweets before tests anymore.
Gina Well, that's funny. That's what happens to me when I drink coffee before _____ important test. Hmmm, maybe next time I won't drink _____ coffee or tea and I will get a better grade!

3 Read about Jaime and Yolanda and answer a–f.

My daily diet: Jaime
I usually drink coffee with milk and I just eat bread and butter for breakfast. For lunch, I eat spaghetti with meat and sometimes chicken with potatoes. For dinner, I usually eat fish with rice or eggs. I sometimes eat an apple after dinner, but I never eat vegetables. I hate them!

My daily diet: Yolanda
I always drink orange juice for breakfast and sometimes I eat an apple. For lunch, I eat fish and some vegetables or salad. In the evening, I usually only have an egg and some fruit, and I often drink tea without milk with my dinner. I only eat chocolate on my birthday!

a What does Jamie normally have for breakfast?
b How often does Jaime eat fruit?
c What food doesn't Jaime like?
d What does Yolanda drink every day?
e What does Yolanda occasionally eat?
f How often does Yolanda eat vegetables or salad?

4 **Make it personal** Write a similar paragraph about your daily diet.

5 ▶ 6.3 Look at the shopping list and talk about the things you have or don't have. Follow the model.

Model: eggs
You: I have some eggs.
Model: milk
You: I don't have any milk.

Connect

Get a classmate to make a video of you talking about your daily diet. Send each other your videos.

6.3 How often do you eat chocolate?

1 ▶ 6.4 Read the blog post and circle the correct forms. Listen to check.

My family
by Hannah King

My mom and dad have a very good diet and are very healthy. They only eat **a little / a few** red meat like pork or beef and they drink **a little / a few** coffee and tea each day. The problem is that my brother and I love fast food. We don't like healthy food and only eat **a little / a few** vegetables such as potatoes or beans. My parents say it is important that we eat fruit and vegetables because they are good for us, so I sometimes eat **a little / a few** apples or bananas. My brother thinks he is healthy because he only eats **a little / a few** chocolate daily and he never drinks coffee or tea, but he does drink a lot of soft drinks!! I don't like soft drinks very much, so I drink **a little / a few** water, but usually I drink tea or juice. I think my brother and I need to eat and drink more healthy food.

💬 13 comments

2 Complete the sentences about the blog post.
   a Hannah's parents want her to eat a _____.
   b Hannah and her brother love _____.
   c Hannah sometimes eats _____ like bananas.
   d Hannah's brother doesn't eat _____ chocolate.

3 Match technical words a–e to their meaning.
   a calorie ⬜ a substance that can block arteries
   b cholesterol ⬜ a chemical element found in salt
   c protein ⬜ a substance in foods such as meat, eggs, and milk that people need to grow
   d sodium ⬜ the parts of fruit, vegetables, and grains that our bodies cannot digest
   e fiber ⬜ a unit used to measure how much energy we get from food

4 Complete extracts a–e from SB units 1–5 with *a few / a little*.
   a I need _____ information from you.
   b No, I don't exercise. I'm _____ lazy.
   c I need to ask you _____ questions.
   d I speak _____ Spanish.
   e Just _____ things to remember: When you come in …

5 🅰 **Make it personal** Complete a–e with *a few / a little / a lot of* so they're true for you. Add a frequency adverb when necessary.
   a I _____ eat _____ bread during the week.
   b I _____ eat _____ calories at lunch time.
   c There are _____ nice places to visit in our country.
   d I _____ travel with _____ money.
   e After lunch, I _____ eat _____ dessert.

6 ▶ 6.5 Answer these questions about Mike. Follow the model.
   Model: *Does Mike buy a lot of potatoes?*
   You: *No, he only buys a few.*
   Model: *Does he buy a lot of coffee?*
   You: *No, he only buys a little.*

6.4 How many meals do you cook a week?

1 ▶ **6.6** Steven is asking Becky about her diet. Listen. True (T) or False (F)?
   a Becky doesn't like any fruit. _____
   b Becky only eats carrots and onions. _____
   c Becky thinks fast food is good for you. _____
   d Becky drinks a little tea every day. _____
   e Steven thinks Becky has an unhealthy diet. _____

2 ▶ **6.6** Order the words to make questions. Listen to check.
   S Excuse me. My school is doing a survey to find out about people's diets. Can I ask you a few questions?
   B Certainly. What do you want to know?
   S ¹healthy / Do / ? / a / have / you / diet
   B I think so.
   S Well, ²fruit / how / do / every / eat / much / day / ? / you
   B Not a lot, I'm afraid. I only eat bananas, I don't like other fruit.
   S OK, so ³bananas / you / do / ? / many / every / eat / how / week
   B Just a few – maybe two or three. But I do eat vegetables.
   S ⁴like / you / all / ? / Do / vegetables
   B Yes, carrots and onions are my favorite.
   S ⁵vegetables / usually / week / you / ? / How / eat / do / many / eat / every
   B Lots – I eat vegetables every day. But I don't eat a lot of meat.
   S ⁶meat / How / ? / eat / do / much / you
   B Well, I usually have a piece of chicken or fish on the weekend, but that's all.
   S OK. What about fast food? ⁷food / ? / much / eat / fast / do / How / you
   B I never eat any fast food. It's so unhealthy.
   S Can I ask you about your drinks now? ⁸day / tea or coffee / many / cups / How / ? / of / every / have / you / do
   B I have two cups of green tea every day, and then I drink water. I don't like coffee.
   S Wow! You have a very healthy diet. ⁹eat / Do / unhealthy / you / ? / anything
   B Well, I do like chocolate cake!
   S And ¹⁰cake / eat / week / chocolate / how / of / ? / many / you / slices / do / every
   B Oh, one every day.
   S Seven slices of chocolate cake every week? That's not very healthy!

3 ▶ **6.7** Listen and complete the ingredients.

   Tasty Tomato Sauce
   2 cans of _____ paste
   1 tablespoon of _____
   1 tablespoon of oregano
   1 teaspoon of _____

   Ingredients:
   2 pounds of _____
   1 _____
   4 cans of _____

   tablespoon   teaspoon

4 Jack and Tracy are going to make the sauce. Complete with *how much*, *how many*, *a few*, *a lot*, or *a little*.
   J Tracy, I have a surprise for you. Tonight I'm making dinner!
   T Sounds wonderful! What are you making?
   J Spaghetti with tomato sauce.
   T Uh, do you need help?
   J Well, maybe you can read the recipe to me. _____ meat do I need?
   T Two pounds.
   J Hmm, we only have _____ meat.
   T Well, how about we don't use meat this time?
   J Good idea. OK. I have _____ cans of tomatoes. _____ cans do we need?
   T Four.
   J Four? That's a lot! I only have two.
   T And _____ tomato paste do you have?
   J Er ... I have _____ cans.
   T OK, we only need two.
   J OK, I have that. _____ onions do I need? I have _____ because I know you love onions.
   T Well, we only need one.
   J Ok, what else? Soup, right? _____ miso soup do I need?
   T Hmm, no, Jack. You don't need any soup for this recipe. But you need _____ oil.
   J Oh, no! I don't have any oil.
   T You know what? Why don't we just call for pizza?

5 ▶ **6.8** Imagine you're going shopping for your family. Ask questions. Follow the model.

   Model: *sugar*
   You: *How much sugar do we need?*
   Model: *bottles of mineral water*
   You: *How many bottles of mineral water do we need?*

6.5 What would you like for lunch?

1 Look at the pictures and complete the puzzle.

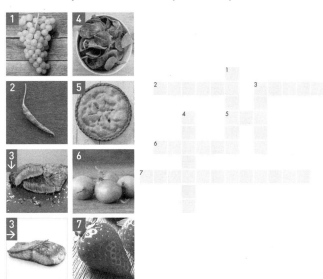

2 Put the words in the correct columns.

main courses   pureed   lettuce   grilled
barbecued   sautéed   steamed
starters   desserts   baked   lemon
melon   pears   carrots   onions

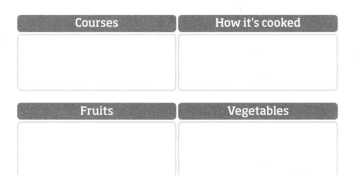

Courses	How it's cooked

Fruits	Vegetables

3 ▶ 6.9 Circle the correct forms. Listen to check.
Liv Hmm, I'm so hungry.
Ned Well, there isn't much in the fridge ... Let's see. **Would you / Do you** like an orange?
Liv Oh, no, thanks. I **wouldn't / don't** like oranges. Do you have any apples?
Ned I think so. **Would you / Do you** like one?
Liv Sure.
Ned Here it is.
Liv Uh, Ned, this apple looks really bad. **I would like / like** apples but not that much.
Ned Oops, sorry about that. Hey, **would you / do you** like some pizza? There's some in the freezer.
Liv No, thanks. I **wouldn't / don't** like any pizza now.
Ned Why not? I thought you really **would like / liked** pizza.
Liv Yeah, but not for breakfast!

4 ▶ 6.10 Order the words in the underlined phrases to complete the restaurant dialogue. Listen to check.
Gary Good evening. Welcome to Tom's Diner. My name is Gary and I'll be your server tonight.
April <u>I / menu / have / can / the</u>, please?
_____
Gary Sure. <u>you / to / a / like / starter / would / order</u>?
_____
April Yes, thanks. <u>the / have / chicken / I'll / salad</u>, please.
_____
Gary <u>drink / anything / to</u>?
_____
April Uh, yes. <u>I / like / soda / diet / a / would</u>, please.
_____
Gary Just a minute, please.
April Oh, excuse me?
Gary Yes?
April <u>you / a / me / could / bring / plate / clean</u>? This one is dirty.
_____
Gary Oh, sure. Sorry about that.
April No problem.

5 ▶ 6.11 Imagine you're at a restaurant. Order some items. Follow the model.
Model: *have – grilled chicken*
You: *I'll have the grilled chicken, please.*
Model: *like – barbecued steak*
You: *I'd like the barbecued steak, please.*
Model: *can – fish fillet*
You: *Can I have the fish fillet, please?*

Connect
Use the dialogue in **4** to practice a similar one with your partner. Record your dialogue and send it to your teacher.

Can you remember ...
▶ 22 food items? SB→p.72
▶ 10 uncountable food items? SB→p.73
▶ 9 countable food items? SB→p.73
▶ 7 portions of food? SB→p.74
▶ 3 quantifiers? SB→p.77
▶ 3 starters, 3 main courses, and 3 desserts? SB→p.80

7

7.1 Do you live in a house?

1 Circle the "different" item in each group. Write the room in the last column.

> basement   bathroom   bedroom
> dining room   garage   kitchen
> living room   office   laundry room

a	(windows)	tools	storage space	basement
b	sink	fireplace	bathtub	
c	armchair	stove	microwave	
d	shelves	computer	oven	
e	closet	bathtub	shelves	
f	TV	bed	sofa	
g	car	bike	fan	
h	table	chairs	shower	
i	dryer	TV	washing machine	

2 Match a–i to a room in **1**.

a This is my _____. It's a little small, but I only come here to sleep.
b Welcome to my favorite room. It's the _____. I love sleeping on the sofa or watching TV here.
c I love cooking, so my favorite room is my _____.
d There's a _____ under the house with a lot of storage space.
e This is the _____. I only come here once a week to wash and dry my clothes.
f I work from home a lot, so I have an _____ with a computer.
g I don't have a _____, so my car is in front of my house.
h The _____ is really small, just a shower and a toilet.
i My parents have dinner parties in the _____, there's space for about eight people to eat.

3 ▶ 7.1 Make sentences. Follow the model.

Model: A sofa. The living room.
You: There's a sofa in the living room.
Model: Some shoes. The bathtub.
You: There are some shoes in the bathtub.

4 🔲 Make it personal Use the sentences in **2** to talk about your own house.

5 Read and answer a–c, True (T) or False (F).

Project Renovation is about individuals who take old, run down buildings and turn them into their ideal home. In tonight's episode, the host Kelly Fogarty visits an ambitious renovation project to talk with a young couple about their new house and film the progress.

a Project Renovation is the name of a TV show.
b It is about groups of people building new houses.
c On tonight's show, the host goes to more than one project.

6 ▶ 7.2 Listen and complete a–d with *was* / *were* ⊕ ⊖.

> In the original house:
> a There _____ bathroom, or toilet, so this is a big part of the project.
> b The toilet _____ in the yard.
> c There _____ a big kitchen.
> d And there _____ windows in the kitchen.

7 ▶ 7.2 Listen again and complete a–f with rooms or furniture.

> Now:
> a Today, they are working on the _____.
> b The bathroom is above the _____.
> c The kitchen and the _____ are together in one room.
> d The _____ and the refrigerator are coming next week.
> e They are using the _____ to cook.
> f Phillip is excited about his new _____.

7.2 Where were you last night?

1 Add vowels to the incomplete words to make common party items.

How to plan the
perfect party!

a Make the <u>invitati o</u>ns and send them early.

b You can decorate the house with colored b__ll__ __ns.

c If it's a birthday, make a c__k__ and put c__ndl__s on it.

d Have lots of sn__ __ks for people to eat.

e You also need drinks like l__m__n__d__ or c__l__.

f Some people like hot drinks so get some c__ff__ __ and t__a.

g Remember to have lots of pl__t__s, n__pk__ns, and gl__ss__s.

h It's a good idea to have f__r__w__rks. Everybody loves them.

i A good party needs good m__s__c!

2 🎤 Make it personal Describe your perfect party.

3 ▶ 7.3 Add one word to questions a–h to make them correct in the past. Listen to check.

a When Mari's party? (was)
b How was?
c Where it?
d What the weather like?
e there a lot of food?
f there fireworks?
g there a cake?
h How many people there at the party?

4 ▶ 7.3 Listen again and repeat the questions.

5 ▶ 7.4 Listen to a conversation and answer the questions in **3**.

6 🎤 Make it personal Write a short note about your last party. Use the questions in **3** to help.

7 Take the music quiz. Match the song lines to the artists.

a "You **were** driving the getaway car."

b "I **was** just an only child of the universe. And then I found you."

c "Yesterday, love **was** such an easy game to play."

d "Listen to me when I say, I'm beautiful in my way because God makes no mistakes. I'm on the right track baby, I **was** born this way."

e "Cause I am whatever you say I am. If I **wasn't** then why would I say I am?"

f "When I **was** six years old, I broke my leg."

g "Look at the stars. Look how they shine for you, and everything you do. Yeah, they **were** all yellow."

h "Once there **was** a way to get back homeward. Once there **was** a way to get back home."

i "If I **were** a boy, even just for a day."

☐ Dua Lipa
☐ The Beatles
☐ Taylor Swift
☐ Coldplay
☐ Eminem
☐ Fall Out Boy
☐ Lady Gaga
☐ Beyonce
☐ Ed Sheeran

📶 **Connect**

*Use the questions in **3** to interview a friend about his / her last party. Record your interview and send it to another pair to listen.*

7.3 Where were you last New Year's Eve?

1 Read the webpage about these events and answer a–c.
a Which event has the most people?
b Which event has music?
c Which event has food that people don't eat?

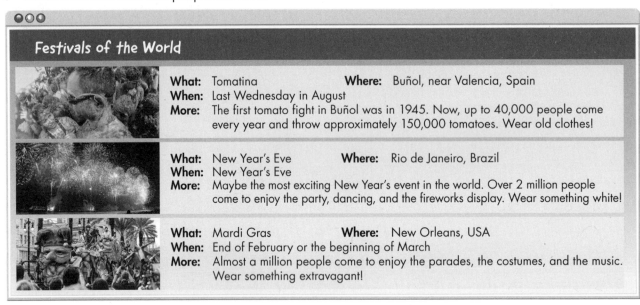

Festivals of the World

What: Tomatina Where: Buñol, near Valencia, Spain
When: Last Wednesday in August
More: The first tomato fight in Buñol was in 1945. Now, up to 40,000 people come every year and throw approximately 150,000 tomatoes. Wear old clothes!

What: New Year's Eve Where: Rio de Janeiro, Brazil
When: New Year's Eve
More: Maybe the most exciting New Year's event in the world. Over 2 million people come to enjoy the party, dancing, and the fireworks display. Wear something white!

What: Mardi Gras Where: New Orleans, USA
When: End of February or the beginning of March
More: Almost a million people come to enjoy the parades, the costumes, and the music. Wear something extravagant!

2 ▶ 7.5 Match the comments to two festivals, then complete them with *was* or *were*. Listen to check.

a January 3, 2018 **Julianne**
That _____ an amazing party! And the fireworks _____ awesome! I love this city!

b September 2, 2018 **Lucas**
I'm still washing my clothes after the festival! It _____ so messy and my shoes _____ ruined, but it _____ good fun.

3 Use the picture to complete the text with these prepositions.

above   behind   ~~between~~   in   in front of   next to   on   across from   under

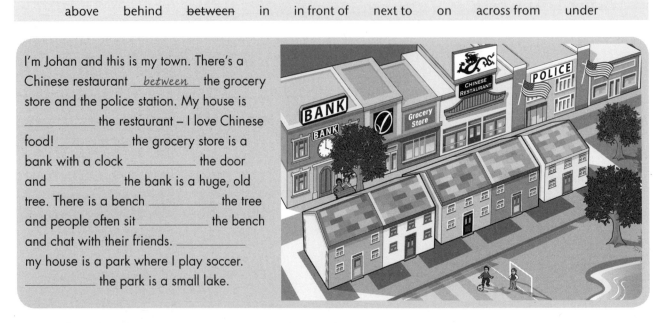

I'm Johan and this is my town. There's a Chinese restaurant _between_ the grocery store and the police station. My house is _____ the restaurant – I love Chinese food! _____ the grocery store is a bank with a clock _____ the door and _____ the bank is a huge, old tree. There is a bench _____ the tree and people often sit _____ the bench and chat with their friends. _____ my house is a park where I play soccer. _____ the park is a small lake.

4 🗣 Make it personal Describe your town to your partner.

7.4 Was your hometown different 10 years ago?

1 ▶ 7.6 Complete a–e with a date. Listen to check. Any surprises?

| 1903 | 1912 | 1972 | 1990 | 2012 | 2016 |

Famous Firsts and Lasts
a Rihanna's *Work* was a #1 international hit in _____.
b The first airplane flight with a pilot was in _____.
c The first successful communication on the Internet was in _____.
d George, the last Galápagos Giant Tortoise, died in _____.
e The Titanic's first, and last, voyage was in _____.
f The last man to walk on the moon was in _____.

2 ▶ 7.7 Look at the two pictures of André's town. Then complete the sentences. Listen to check.

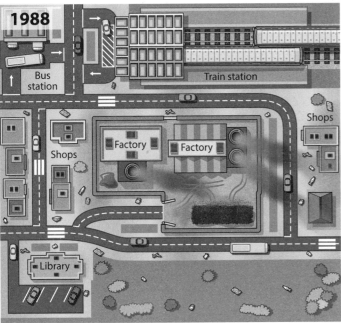
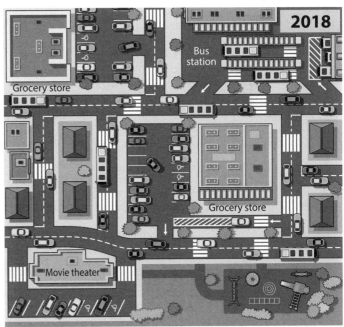

1988
There _were_ a few cars.
There _____ a train station and a bus station.
There _____ a grocery store.
There _____ a library next to the park.
There _____ two factories.
There _____ a play area for children in the park.
There _____ any big roads.
The town _____ very dirty.

Today
There _____ a lot of cars.
There _____ a train station. There _____ a big bus station.
There _____ two grocery stores.
There _____ a library, but there _____ a movie theater.
There _____ any factories.
There _____ now a big play area in the park.
There _____ a lot of new roads.
The town _____ dirty now. It is clean and beautiful.

3 🗣 **Make it personal** Are a–e True (T) or False (F) for your town?
a There were trains here fifty years ago.
b There was a lot of pollution, but it's clean now.
c There were a lot more small stores a few years ago.
d There wasn't anywhere for children to play, but now there are some play areas.
e There were some beautiful old buildings, but they aren't there now.

7.5 How about a barbecue on Sunday?

1 Read the article and answer a–d.
   a Where is Glastonbury?
   b When is the festival?
   c What kind of festival is it?
   d How can you buy a ticket?

GLASTONBURY FESTIVAL

Glastonbury is a small, old, historical town in the heart of southwest England. But every summer, at the end of June, around a quarter of a million people arrive there to celebrate the Glastonbury Festival, making it one of the 20 biggest cities in Britain. The world-famous music and arts festival has something for everybody, and some very big stars. To many people it is simply the best festival in the world. There was no festival in 2018, but the 2017 festival was fabulous, as usual. To get a ticket for next year register online at www.glastonburyfestivals.co.uk.

2 ▶ 7.8 Listen and match the numbers to the phrases to make statistics for Glastonbury 2016. Listen again to check.

30	days
5	minutes to sell all the tickets
60	people in the audience
1,300	performances
Over 2,200	recycling volunteers
5,489	stages
220,000	toilets

3 ▶ 7.8 Listen again and write down three more numbers from the audio. What do they refer to?

4 ▶ 7.9 Circle the correct word in invitations a–f. Then listen and complete with these phrases.

| a barbecue | a soccer game | a party |
| a restaurant | the movies | the park |

a Would you like **to go** / **going** to _____?
b Do you **want** / **like** to go to _____ this weekend?
c **Do** / **Would** you like to come to _____ on Saturday?
d How about **go** / **going** to _____ after lunch?
e I'm having _____ on Friday. Can you **make** / **do** it?
f We're going to _____ for our 25th wedding anniversary. Can you **go** / **come**?

🔗 Connect

Choose an event from **4**. Send a message to a friend to invite them to your event.

Can you remember ...

▸ 9 rooms in a house? SB→p. 86
▸ 16 items of furniture? SB→p. 86
▸ 15 things you need for a party? SB→p. 88
▸ 9 prepositions of place? SB→p. 91
▸ how to talk about changes in a town? SB→p. 93
▸ how to invite a friend to a party? SB→p. 95

8.1 When did you start school?

1 **Complete sentences a–h with the correct form of these verbs.**

agreed	died	learned	married
started	studied	wanted	worked

a My parents got _____ in 1989. My mom wore a beautiful white dress.
b My sister _____ to drive a car last year. She isn't very good!!
c I like to help people, so I _____ to wash the car.
d Nelson Mandela _____ in 2013 in South Africa.
e We _____ to have a barbecue in the yard but it rained.
f Rihanna _____ singing when she was seven years old.
g Dominic _____ engineering at college.
h Hugh Jackman _____ as a physical education teacher before acting.

2 ▶8.1 **Read the biography and circle the correct verb forms. Listen to check.**

Robin Williams **borned / was born** on July 21, 1951 in Chicago. His great-grandfather was a politician in Mississippi, but his parents **weren't / wasn't** interested in politics. His father **worked / work** for Ford Motor Company and his mother **helps / helped** at the church.

Williams **study / studied** political science but didn't like it very much and **move / moved** to Julliard School in New York City to study theater. He **started / start** to work as a stand-up comedian in California and in 1978 **joined / join** the TV show Mork and Mindy as Mork.

By the 1980s, children all over the world **love / loved** him because his movies **was / were** so funny – movies like Mrs. Doubtfire, Happy Feet and Boulevard. However, he didn't just make comedy movies. Williams **play / played** roles in dramatic movies such as Good Morning, Vietnam and Good Will Hunting. He often didn't **follow / followed** a script but **invent / invented** his own dialogue and directors **was / were** happy to let him.

In 1998, Entertainment Weekly **list / listed** him as one of the 25 best actors in the world and he **receive / received** a Star on the Hollywood Walk of Fame on December 12, 1990.

He **loves / loved** sports and **was / were** a big fan of Rugby Union, and he often **watched / watch** the New Zealand All Blacks team. He also **enjoys / enjoyed** cycling and owned 87 bicycles.

He **married / marries** three times and **has / had** three children: Zachary, Zelda, and Cody. Cody **follow / followed** his father into the movie industry and is now an assistant director.

Robin Williams **die / died** on August 11, 2014 at home in California. He was 63 years old.

3 **Reread the biography. True (T), False (F) or Not Given (NG)?**

a Robin Williams' great-grandfather worked in politics.
b His first job was on a TV show.
c He was only famous for his comedy roles.
d Robin Williams enjoyed playing Rugby Union.
e He got married more than once.
f Williams' son Cody is an actor, too.

4 ▶8.2 **Listen and make sentences about Joe. Follow the model.**

Model: *study English / last weekend*
You: *Joe studied English last weekend.*
Model: *start school / in 1990*
You: *Joe started school in 1990.*

5 **Write Whitney Houston's biography using the information in a–g.**

a born / August 9, 1963 / Newark, New Jersey
_____
b record / her first album / 1985
_____
c receive / her first Grammy / 1986
_____
d married / Bobby Brown / July 18, 1992
_____
e star in the movie The Bodyguard / 1992
_____
f produce / the movie Sparks / September 2011
_____
g die / in a hotel / February 9, 2012
_____

8.2 Did you go out last weekend?

1 Read about Mia and circle 18 past tense verbs. Put them in the correct spelling rules box.

When Mia finished school, she wanted to travel. She took a gap year, studied a map of the world, and decided to go to South East Asia. Before she left her parents gave her a new camera to record all the wonderful things she saw. She flew to Indonesia in May, and when she arrived she sailed to Sumatra and got a job as a volunteer in the rainforest. She helped in a park looking after orangutans. She stayed for six months and made lots of new friends. They all cried when she said good-bye!
She had a fantastic time in Indonesia and wants to go back there again one day.

1 - Most regular verbs	2 - Verbs ending in -e	3 - Verbs ending in consonant + y	4 - Irregular verbs
		cried	

2 Now put these verbs in the past and add them to the boxes in 1.

buy   come   do   go   invite   know   play   start   think   try   use

3 ▶8.3 Circle the correct preposition. Then listen to check.

Bob Marley was born **on / in** February 6, 1945 **on / in** the village of Nine Mile in Jamaica. He left school **at / in** the age **for / of** 14 to make music. **On / In** 1962, he recorded his first two singles, but the songs didn't attract a lot of attention. With his stepbrother and some friends, he created the band The Wailers **in / on** 1963. **On / In** 1966, he married Rita Anderson. The Wailers only released their first major album **at / in** April of 1973. **On / In** July, 1977, doctors discovered that Marley had cancer. He still released a new album **in / on** May 1980. He died at a hospital in Miami **in / on** May 11, 1981.

4 Complete with the correct ordinal number.
  a Bob Marley's _____ (2) name was Robert.
  b Ziggy is his _____ (1) child.
  c His _____ (11) child, Damian, was born on July _____ (21), 1978.
  d His final concert happened on September _____ (23), 1980, in Pittsburgh.
  e In 1999, *Time* magazine chose The Wailers' *Exodus* as the best album of the _____ (20) century.

5 ▶8.4 Look at the birthdates of these singers and answer the questions. Follow the model.
  Model: *When was Elvis Presley born?*   You: *He was born on January 8th, 1935.*

8.3 Where did you go on your last vacation?

1 ▶8.5 **Make it personal** Notice the pronunciation of *did you* (/dɪdʒə/). Listen and repeat. Listen again and answer.
   a   What *did you* do last weekend?
   b   What time *did you* get up on Sunday?
   c   What *did you* eat?
   d   Who *did you* see?
   e   Where *did you* go?
   f   *Did you* go to the movies?
   g   *Did you* stay at home?
   h   *Did you* have a good time?

2 Imagine a friend went to Paris on vacation. Write questions for the underlined parts of the sentences.
   a   _____?
       I went with <u>my family</u>.
   b   _____?
       We stayed <u>at the Hôtel San Régis</u>.
   c   _____?
       <u>Yes, we did</u>. We met a nice couple from Finland.
   d   _____?
       <u>No, we didn't</u>. We don't usually take a lot of photos.
   e   _____?
       We bought <u>souvenirs and perfume</u>.

3 Reread the interview on SB p. 103. Correct the information about Ms. Riggs' trip.
   a   She went to Turkey with her husband.
       She didn't go with her husband. She went alone.
   b   She went to Turkey on vacation.
       _____
   c   She took a plane to Cappadocia.
       _____
   d   The trip to Cappadocia took six hours.
       _____
   e   They stopped at a restaurant in Istanbul.
       _____
   f   They ate Japanese food.
       _____
   g   She didn't like the trip.
       _____

Connect
Use the questions in 1 to interview a friend about his / her weekend. Record your interview and send it to a classmate or your teacher.

4 ▶8.6 Use the information below and correct these sentences. Emphasize the part you're correcting. Follow the model.

   Model: *She had a train ticket to Cappadocia.*
   You: *She didn't have a **train** ticket. She had a **plane** ticket.*
   a   plane ticket
   b   a ride
   c   Turkish food
   d   interesting places
   e   great time

5 ▶8.7 Read the blog. Use the verbs in bold in the past tense to complete the puzzle below. Listen to check.

Mike Mozey

Last weekend my girlfriend **say** (3) she wanted to go to a different place. So I **make** (2↓) a reservation for dinner at a new restaurant in town. We **go** (7) in separate cars and **meet** (2→) there.
The food was really great. We **eat** (1) good Italian pasta and **drink** (6) a bottle of soda.
At the end, when the check **come** (4), we got a big surprise: it was only one dollar!
I **know** (5) that was wrong so I called the manager. The manager **say** (3) that we were their 1,000th client, so that was a gift for us. It was perfect!

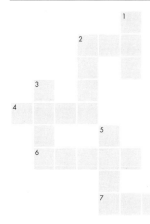

6 Answer a–d about the blog in 5.
   a   Why did they go to a new restaurant?
   b   Did they go to the restaurant together?
   c   How much did they pay for dinner?
   d   Why did they pay that much?

8.4 When do you listen to music?

1 ▶ 8.8 Listen to this interview with singer Ginny Lomond, and check the actions she mentions.

1	2	3
start school	record first album	move to Los Angeles
go to school	record second album	move to New York
leave school	record last album	move to Paris

2 ▶ 8.8 Listen again and answer questions a–f about the interview.
   a When did she start her career?
   b Where did she study?
   c Where was Ginny born?
   d Who moved to New York?
   e Was her first album a success?
   f When did she record her second album?

3 Ask questions for the underlined part of the sentences.

   a _____?
      Time Magazine elects the 100 most influential people every year.

   b _____?
      Angelina Jolie divorced <u>Brad Pitt</u> in 2016.

   c _____?
      <u>Tom Ford</u> studied fashion design in the 1990s.

   d _____?
      <u>Serena Williams</u> won four Olympic gold medals in tennis.

   e _____?
      Steven Spielberg met <u>Kate Capshaw</u> while filming the second *Indiana Jones* movie.

   f _____?
      Ryan Gosling moved to <u>Los Angeles</u> in 1996.

4 ▶ 8.9 Look back at Jake's morning routine on SB p. 20 and tell it in the past. Listen to check.

   > Yesterday Jake woke up at …

5 🗣 **Make it personal** What did you do yesterday?

   > I woke up early and …

8.5 Could you help me, please?

1 ▶ 8.10 Read the email and correct the 14 mistakes. The numbers show how many mistakes per line. Listen to check.

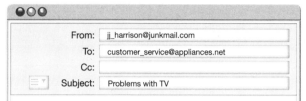

To Customer Service,

I ~~buyed~~ bought a new 40" flat screen TV from your 1
store on June 12 this year. And I regret this
decision every single day …

The delivery were late. Instead of three days, 1
I haved to wait one week. But then I finally 1
get my TV. To my surprise, the sound didn't 1
worked. The image was beautiful, but 1
there were only noise. So I called technical 1
support. A person come and he sayed the 2
TV needed a new part, but he didn't had it 1
there.

That was two weeks ago. I called technical
support again but they didn't knew anything 1
about the part. So another repairperson
came, look at the TV, sayed that he didn't 2
haved the necessary part, and left – without 1
fixing the TV again.

That was one week ago. Now I'm afraid of
calling technical support again and getting
another useless visit. Could you please
helped me? Could you please check the 1
reports from your repairmen and make sure
the next one brings the necessary part?

Thank you very much.

James J. Harrison

2 **Reread. True (T) or False (F)?**
  a The buyer is happy that he bought this TV.
  b The delivery took 7 days, not 3 as promised.
  c The image of the TV was perfect.
  d The repairmen couldn't repair the TV because they didn't have the proper part.
  e Three different repairmen came to his house.

3 🅐 **Make it personal** Use the information below to write an email like the one in **1**. Add more details. Send it to your teacher or a friend.

new cell phone
battery only lasts 15 minutes
tried recharging it
doesn't work
called support
got a new battery
same problem
called technical support again
promised a solution
no solution
a new phone

4 ▶ 8.11 Complete requests a–i with these verbs. Listen to check and repeat each request. Be careful with the pronunciation of **could you** /kʊdʒə/ and **could I** /kʊdaɪ/.

| borrow | have | help | hold | lend |
| open | pass | speak | use | |

  a Could you _____ the window, please?
  b Could you please _____ me the salt?
  c Could you _____ the door, please?
  d Could you please _____ me your phone?
  e Could you _____ me, please?
  f Could I _____ your bathroom, please?
  g Could I _____ your pen, please?
  h Could I _____ the menu, please?
  i Could I _____ to Mr. Green, please?

5 ▶ 8.11 Listen again and note the replies.

📶 Connect

*Use your phone to record yourself making the requests in **4**. Send the recording to your teacher.*

Can you remember …

▸ 10 verb phrases from Maud's biography? SB▸p. 98
▸ 3 spelling rules for the simple past formation? SB▸p. 99
▸ the auxiliary verb for the simple past? SB▸p. 100
▸ 14 common irregular verbs in the simple past? SB▸p. 100
▸ ordinal numbers 1–31? SB▸p. 101
▸ 8 questions about past events? SB▸p. 102
▸ 10 actions from Jay De La Fuente's daily routine? SB▸p. 104
▸ 4 phone problems? SB▸p. 106
▸ 7 favors and responses? SB▸p. 107

9

9.1 How did you get here today?

1 Match the types of transportation to descriptions a–j.

- [ ] a bike
- [ ] a bus
- [ ] a car
- [ ] a ferry
- [ ] on foot
- [a] a helicopter
- [ ] a motorcycle
- [ ] a plane
- [ ] a train
- [ ] a truck

a A flying machine that is popular with the police.
b It has four wheels and is for two to five people.
c A big flying machine that makes global tourism easy.
d It travels on the road and carries many people.
e A large road vehicle that carries heavy cargo.
f A boat that carries passengers and cars.
g A vehicle with two wheels. You power it with your legs.
h Public transportation invented in England in the 19th century.
i It's like a bike, but it has a motor.
j When you walk, you travel …

2 ▶ 9.1 Which of the underlined letters has a different sound?

a t**oo**k   fl**ew**   f**oo**t
b l**o**ved   dr**o**ve   r**o**de
c b**i**ke   b**i**g   r**i**de
d h**ou**r   h**ou**se   h**e**licopter
e f**e**rry   tr**ai**n   c**a**me

3 Complete 1–3 with the past form of the verb.
1 A What did you do on your vacation?
   B I _rented_ (rent) a car and _____ (drive) from New York to Las Vegas.
   A Wow! How did you get to New York?
   B I _____ (fly) with YouAir, the food was great!
2 A Your face is red, are you OK?
   B I'm hot! I _____ (ride) my bike here.
3 A Sorry, I'm late. I _____ (take) the train and there was a problem with the line.
   B I heard about that. I _____ (come) by bus. The traffic was terrible!

4 ▶ 9.2 Complete the dialogue with these words. Listen to check.

| accident | delayed | flat tire | late |
| traffic jam | wrong turn | | |

1 A Why are you so late?
   B There was a terrible _____ on the highway. We waited for two hours!
   A Oh, no. Was there an _____?
   B Yes, I think so. There was a police helicopter there.
2 A Where's Tom?
   B Oh, he called and said his car had a _____ so he took a train.
   A OK, so where is he?
   B The train was _____! He's walking from the station now.
3 A Was your flight _____ yesterday?
   B No, why?
   A Well you got here very late.
   B Ah that's because the taxi driver made a _____!

5 Read about Isabella and her family and correct the six mistakes.

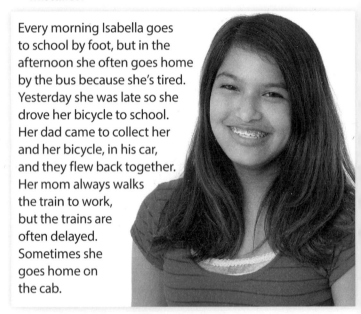

Every morning Isabella goes to school by foot, but in the afternoon she often goes home by the bus because she's tired. Yesterday she was late so she drove her bicycle to school. Her dad came to collect her and her bicycle, in his car, and they flew back together. Her mom always walks the train to work, but the trains are often delayed. Sometimes she goes home on the cab.

6 🎧 Make it personal Order the words in a–f to make questions. Write short answers to them.

a to / did / class / you / ? / get / how
  How did you get to class?   On foot.
b do / you / work / ? / to / usually / get / how
  _____
c you / do / school / ? / the / bus / to / take
  _____
d ? / ride / motorcycle / a / you / can
  _____
e you / usually / supermarket / ? / to / the / get / do / how
  _____
f your / way / ? / to / what / travel / 's / favorite
  _____

7 ▶ 9.3 Practice the sentences. Follow the model.

Model: _I flew / plane._   Model: _She walked / foot._
You: _I came by plane._   You: _She came on foot._

44

9.2 What do you do?

1 Read the magazine article and answer a–e.

Almost everybody hates their commute. The bus or the train is full of people, or there is a lot of traffic on the road. For most people, commuting is uncomfortable and boring, but at least it is safe. For the residents of Los Pinos, Colombia, things are a little different. People in the village have a choice of a two-hour walk through the mountains or a one-minute trip on a zip-line across the canyon that separates their homes from the rest of the world. There are two cables across the valley, one to get out and one to get back. They are four hundred meters long and three hundred and fifty meters high and you can go over 60 kilometers per hour! Very young children use the zip-line to get to school and their parents use it to take products to market. The government doesn't want to build a bridge because not many people live in the village.

a According to the article, what is one positive thing about the average commute?
b How long does it take to walk through the mountains?
c Do villagers use the same zip-line to go to and from the village?
d Are there any age restrictions on using the zip-line?
e Are the authorities planning to build a bridge?

2 Match words a–e from the article to the definitions.

a to commute
b a village
c a trip
d a cable
e to build

☐ a large, strong line made of metal that connects two points
☐ an excursion, a voyage, or a journey
☐ to construct
☐ a small community
☐ to travel regularly to the same place

3 Complete the puzzle with professions. Example: O = 👁.

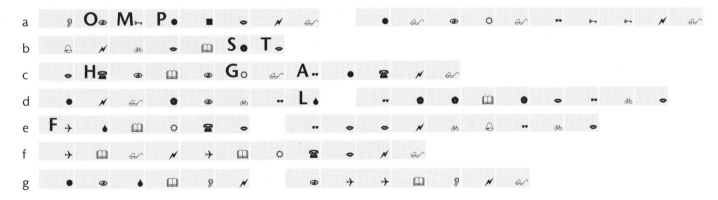

4 ▶ 9.4 Listen to check. Write the seven questions you hear.

5 🎧 Make it personal Check the jobs in **3** that make a lot of money and circle the dangerous jobs.

6 ▶ 9.5 Practice the sentences. Follow the model.

Model: *cook / they*
You: *They are cooks.*

Model: *dentist / I*
You: *I'm a dentist.*

9.3 Where are you going to be in 2025?

1 **Correct the mistakes in a–f.**
   a What time you going to finish work tomorrow?
   b Which team going to win the next World Cup?
   c When are you go to go on your next vacation?
   d Where are you going have lunch tomorrow?
   e You are going to do your homework?
   f What are you go to do next weekend?

2 ▶ **9.6 Listen to 1–6 and circle the pronunciation you hear. Match them to questions a–f in 1.**
   1 I'm **going to** / **gonna** have lunch in a restaurant.
   2 I'm **going to** / **gonna** stay home.
   3 No. I'm not **going to** / **gonna** have time. I have to work tonight.
   4 I'm **going to** / **gonna** finish early today, about 5 o'clock.
   5 We're **going to** / **gonna** go on vacation at Christmas.
   6 I think France is **going to** / **gonna** win the next World Cup.

Connect
Use your phone to record your answers. Send them to your teacher or a friend.

3 **Make it personal** Answer the questions in **1**.

4 Read the article and match the predictions to the pictures.

Once upon a time the 21st century was the future. This is how people imagined it.

In 1909 people predicted this: "in the future all important cities are going to have a roof to protect them against rain and snow."

In 1939 a newspaper made this prediction: "in the future we are going to have light-weight, solar-powered cars. We are not going to need garages because people are going to fold their cars and store them under the bed."

There are a lot of predictions about cheap and easy air travel. This is an example from the 1960s. "In the future everyone is going to have a flying car. Travel is going to be very easy and very cheap."

5 **Reread. True (T) or False (F) according to the predictions?**
   a People are going to keep their cars in the house.
   b Cars in the future are going to use the sun for power.
   c All cities in the future are going to have a roof.
   d It isn't going to snow in the future.
   e Flying cars are going to be expensive.

9.4 What are you going to do next year?

1 Cross out the item that *doesn't* collocate with the verb. Which two aren't usually life changes?

   a Get   ~~college~~ / married / divorced
   b Leave   college / home / house
   c Start   a new job / a friend / a family
   d Move   house / engaged / your car
   e Lose   a job / a train / your keys
   f Find   married / a partner / a job

2 Read the article. True (T) or False (F)?

Resolutions—Make or Break

Everywhere, everybody celebrates the New Year! And we all do it in different ways, but there's one ritual that's common in many cultures: New Year's resolutions. We love them!
But how long do our resolutions usually last? A new study in the U.S. shows that after two weeks 64% of people still keep their resolutions and six months later over 40% still keep their resolutions. Not bad, huh!
So, the BIG question is ... what's the secret to success? And the answer is ... planning! Yes, plan your resolution, tell your friends about it, keep a journal and stay positive. That's your best chance of success!

You can make a resolution at any time of year, not just January 1st! Do you have any resolutions? Follow the advice in the article, make a plan and keep a journal—in English!

   a Many nationalities make resolutions at New Year.
   b Most people keep their resolutions for half a month.
   c Only a few people keep their resolutions after June.
   d Nobody has any advice to help keep a resolution.
   e You should keep your resolutions secret.

3 ▶ 9.7 Match resolutions a–f with the plans. Listen to check.

   a I'm going to get fit and exercise more, so
   b I'm going to save money.
   c I'm going to be more organized.
   d I'm going to volunteer.
   e I'm going to eat better.
   f I'm going to try and relax more.

   ☐ First, I'm going to write a list. Number one ... um?
   ☐ I'm taking cooking classes in the evening.
   ☐ I'm not going to buy unnecessary clothes.
   ☐ I'm going on vacation next month.
   ☐ next week I'm joining a gym.
   ☐ My friend and I are helping at a homeless shelter next week.

4 Read the sentences again. What verb structures do these sentences have? Which ones are about plans with another person or organization?

5 ▶ 9.8 Practice the sentences. Follow the model.

   Model: *save money next year / she*
   You: *She's going to save money next year.*
   Model: *find a new job tomorrow / I*
   You: *I'm going to find a new job tomorrow.*

6 **Make it personal** Write about your plans for next year.

9.5 Would you like to be a nurse?

1 Read and match skills a–e to the reasons.

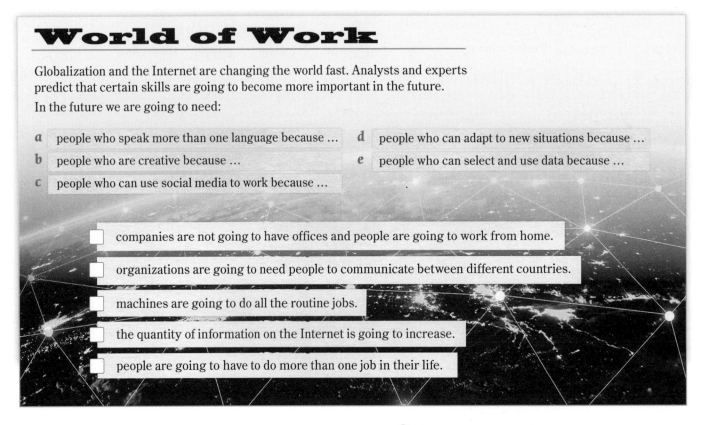

World of Work

Globalization and the Internet are changing the world fast. Analysts and experts predict that certain skills are going to become more important in the future.
In the future we are going to need:

a people who speak more than one language because …
b people who are creative because …
c people who can use social media to work because …
d people who can adapt to new situations because …
e people who can select and use data because …

- companies are not going to have offices and people are going to work from home.
- organizations are going to need people to communicate between different countries.
- machines are going to do all the routine jobs.
- the quantity of information on the Internet is going to increase.
- people are going to have to do more than one job in their life.

2 Check the skills you have, a–e, in **1**.

3 ▶ 9.9 Order the conversation, 1–7. Listen to check. Who's the boss, A or B?

A Fine, thank you. Listen, can I ask you something? ☐
A Oh. OK. ☐
B Sure. Go ahead. ☐
A Hi, how are you? [1]
A Is it OK if I take the day off on Friday? ☐
B Friday? I'm really sorry, but I'm going to go to a meeting on Friday and I really need you here. ☐
B Good, thanks, you? ☐

4 ▶ 9.10 Order the words in a–f to make questions, then complete them with these words. Listen to check.

air conditioning   money   car
sit   question   photo

a I / the / ? / could / _____ / borrow / please
b I / ask / ? / you / a / can / _____
c ? / you / some / could / _____ / me / lend
d if / it / off / OK / I / is / turn / ? / the / _____
e mind / you / ? / if / I / do / _____ / here
f ? / you / your / mind / if / I / do / take / _____

5 ▶ 9.10 Listen again and repeat the questions.

6 ▶ 9.11 Listen to the complete dialogues. Check or cross a–f in **4** when they accept or don't accept.

7 ▶ 9.12 Practice the questions. Follow the model.

Model: *borrow the car / I / can*
You: *Can I borrow the car?*
Model: *open the window / I / mind*
You: *Do you mind if I open the window?*

Can you remember …

- 10 means of transportation and the past verbs for them? SB▸p.112
- 10 jobs? SB▸p.115
- 11 important life changes? SB▸p.118
- 2 ways to talk about plans? SB▸p.119
- 6 important jobs for the future? SB▸p.120
- the difference between *borrow* and *lend*? SB▸p.121
- how to ask permission with *could*? SB▸p.121

10.1 Do you look like your mom?

1 Use the codes chart to find parts of the face, a–e. Then answer the secret question.

	1	2	3	4
A	a	b	c	d
B	e	f	g	h
C	i	k	l	m
D	n	o	p	r
E	s	t	u	y

E.g.: h a i r
      B4 A1 C1 D4

a C4, D2, E3, E2, B4
b B1, E4, B1, E1
c B1, A1, D4, E1
d C3, C1, D3, E1
e D1, D2, E1, B1

_ _ _ _   _ _   _ _ _ _   _ _ _ _   _ _ _ _   _
A4 D2   E4 D2 E3   C3 D2 D2 C2   C3 C1 C2 B1   A1

_ _ _ _ _   _ _ _ _ _ ?
B2 A1 C4 D2 E3 E1   D3 B1 D4 E1 D2 D1

2 Add the words in **1** to groups a–e and cross out the odd word.

a kiss, see, lipstick, smile, _____
b screens, watch, talk, photos, _____
c TV, food, eat, speak, _____
d radio, listen, music, read, _____
e perfume, movies, breathe, smell, _____

3 Complete labels a–j in the picture.

a b a c k
b c _ _ s _
c f _ _ g _ _ s
d _ ee _
e _ _ n _ s
f l _ g _
g s _ _ m _ c _
h _ _ a _
i a _ m _
j t _ _ _ h

4 ▶ 10.1 Complete descriptions a–e about the people in **3**, using these phrases. Listen to check.

| average build | average height | fair hair | long dark hair | old |
| overweight | short gray hair | slim | tall | young |

a Amy is about 45 and has _____. She's Jay's daughter.
b Carmen is from Colombia. She's _____ and _____. She has _____.
c Jay is married to Carmen. He's _____ and he has _____.
d Joseph is Jay's son. He's _____ and _____.
e Cameron is Joseph's partner. She's _____ and _____.

5 ▶ 10.2 Practice the descriptions. Follow the model.

Model: Amy / fair hair
You: This is Amy. She has fair hair.

Model: Carmen / slim / long dark hair
You: This is Carmen. She's slim and has long dark hair.

6 **Make it personal** Email a photo of friends / family to your teacher or a classmate and describe one person in the photo. Can they guess who the person is?

10.2 Are you like your dad?

1 Read the article and complete the chart with three more similarities and three differences between Nick and his dad.

Nick Johnson is 34 and a successful author. He writes suspense novels and his most recent book is The Dark Forest. Here he tells us about the influence of his father.
My father certainly inspired me to be a writer. He loves reading, and he always read to me when I was a child—all kinds of books, newspapers, poems, everything. I think that's why I love reading so much now. My father invented stories for me and my brother when we were young, and sometimes he wrote them so he didn't forget. I keep them in my office now and I still read them.
I wrote my first story when I was nine, but really I copied it from one of my father's. My teacher at school didn't know that and she gave me a good grade! Of course, I write stories now and publish them. Unfortunately, my father never published his. I think I'm going to publish them for him one day, before he dies.
Physically we are a little different. We are both tall, but I'm a little taller than he is. He has fair hair but mine is dark, like my mother's. He was very athletic and really strong when he was younger, he played a lot of sports, but I am not athletic at all.

Similarities	Differences
They both love reading.	

2 Correct two mistakes in each of a–g.

a I am more tall that my brother.
b The weather is badder then yesterday.
c My English is more good than a year before.
d My sister is intelligenter then me.
e Childrens are more happy than adults.
f Dogs are friendlyer that cats.
g My grandmother is generouser then my mom.

3 ▶ 10.3 Listen to the descriptions and label the players in the picture.

Michael   Lewis
Phil   Peter
Steve   Rory
Frank   Wayne

4 Compare the players. Use each word only once.

| happy | intelligent | overweight | ~~short~~ |
| slim | strong | tall | young |

a Rory / Phil   *Rory is shorter than Phil.*
b Lewis / Peter
c Michael / Steve
d Peter / Wayne
e Phil / Lewis
f Wayne / Phil
g Steve / Rory
h Frank / Steve

5 ▶ 10.4 Practice the comparatives. Follow the model.

Model: *Miami / hot / New York*
You: *Miami is hotter than New York.*
Model: *swimming / interesting / fishing*
You: *Swimming is more interesting than fishing.*

10.3 Who's the most generous person in your family?

1 ▶ 10.5 Listen to the adjectives in 1–5 and check the syllable / stress pattern they follow, a–e.
   E.g.: **cri** ti cal = a
   a ●●●   b ●●●●   c ●●●●   d ●●●   e ●●
   ☐ 1   ☐ 2   ☐ 3   ☐ 4   ☐ 5

2 Which word in each group a–d has a different sound pattern?
   a possessive, arrogant, negative, solitary
   b responsible, idealistic, perfectionist, disorganized
   c calm, moody, loyal, angry
   d suspicious, spontaneous, generous, romantic

3 Read the messages from a dating website and match the people together.

a	b	c	d	e	f
Hi, I'm female, 45. I work a lot, but I enjoy life. Want to meet a man to share all I have.	Mario, 26. Tall, dark, romantic Italian. Want to meet a lady to travel the world with.	Hi, Camilla here. I'm ambitious and a perfectionist. Want to meet a similar, successful man!	Steve, 39. Successful businessman wants to meet determined, organized woman.	Hi, I'm Lisa, 24. Want to meet Prince Charming. Buy me flowers and sing to me in Venice!	Male, 35. Fun and relaxed. Not working at the moment. Want to meet a generous lady.

4 🅰 **Make it personal** Change the adjectives to superlatives and add them to the questions. Then answer a–g.
   a Who's _____ person you know? (**crazy**)
   b What's _____ program on TV? (**bad**)
   c Who's _____ person in your family? (**old**)
   d Where's _____ supermarket? (**big**)
   e Which is _____ soccer team in your country? (**popular**)
   f Who's _____ person in your country's history? (**famous**)
   g What's _____ word to pronounce in English? (**difficult**)

5 ▶ 10.6 Complete a–e with these words. Listen to check.

   can   nightclub   park   subway station   thing

   a Excuse me, I need to get to the city center. Where's the nearest _____?
   b Wow, there are so many trees here! Is this the biggest _____ in the city?
   c What's the most important _____ in the museum?
   d So, let's go dancing tonight. What's the best _____ in the city?
   e Which is your cheapest _____ of soda?

6 ▶ 10.6 Listen again. True (T) or False (F)?
   a The subway station is next to the shopping mall.
   b Green Park is next to the river.
   c The most important artifact in the museum is on the third floor.
   d They are in *Venom* now.
   e The cheapest soda is only $2.

📶 Connect
Use your phone to record your answers. Send them to your teacher or a friend.

10.4 What's the best place in the world?

1 ▶ 10.7 Complete facts A–E. Listen to check.

FUN FACTS

A Lake Superior _____ _____ biggest lake _____ _____ world.
B Aconcagua is the _____ _____ in _____ America.
C _____ _____ trees _____ _____ world _____ _____ giant Redwoods _____ California.
D Dolphins _____ more intelligent _____ monkeys.
E Tokyo _____ _____ _____ populated city _____ Asia.

2 ▶ 10.8 Practice the superlatives. Follow the model.

Model: Sally / good singer / the city
You: Sally is the best singer in the city.

Model: Istanbul / beautiful city / the world
You: Istanbul is the most beautiful city in the world.

3 Look at the postcards. Where can you see a–h?

a a big canyon   Arizona
b a beautiful island _____
c a small lake   _____
d an ugly lizard   _____
e a high mountain   _____
f large rocks   _____
g an extinct volcano _____
h a fantastic waterfall _____

4 ▶ 10.9 Listen to Mary and Tess talk about vacations. Answer a–c.
a When did Mary go on vacation?
b Did Mary go to Arizona, Madeira, or Indonesia?
c Where is Tess going to go for her vacation?

5 ▶ 10.9 Listen again. True (T) or False (F)?
a Tess is probably not Mary's boss.
b Mary likes active vacations.
c Tess likes lizards.
d It was sunny every day on Mary's vacation.
e Tess is going on vacation next week.

10.5 Is your English better than a year ago?

1 ▶ 10.10 Do the quiz. Order facts A–E. Circle the correct word in F–J. Listen to check. How many did you get right?

- A HAVE / BLONDES / PEOPLE WITH DARK HAIR / THAN / MORE HAIR / .
- B FASTER / FORMULA ONE CARS / NERVE IMPULSES / THAN / CAN TRAVEL / .
- C THAN / THICKER / MEN'S HAIR / WOMEN'S HAIR / IS / .
- D IS / THAN / A SOCCER FIELD / A FOOTBALL FIELD / BIGGER / .
- E THAN / IS / AN AVERAGE PERSON / HEAVIER / A DOLPHIN / .
- F YOUR HEARING IS **BETTER / WORSE** AFTER YOU EAT.
- G WOMEN HAVE A **STRONGER / WEAKER** SENSE OF SMELL THAN MEN.
- H MONDAY IS THE **SAFEST / MOST DANGEROUS** DAY OF THE WEEK.
- I WE ARE **TALLER / SHORTER** IN THE MORNING.
- J THE HEART BEATS **SLOWER / FASTER** WHEN YOU SLEEP.

2 ▶ 10.11 Listen and answer a–c.
- a When is the fight?
- b Which person is David Silver and which is Danny Belching?
- c Did Danny win his last fight?

3 ▶ 10.11 Listen again and complete descriptions a–g.
- a Danny Belching is s_____ than David Silver.
- b Danny Belching d_____ get t_____.
- c David Silver is t_____ than Danny Belching.
- d David Silver has l_____ a_____.
- e David Silver h_____ a b_____ technique.
- f Danny is a l_____ f_____ than David Silver.
- g Danny w_____ his last t_____ fights.

4 **Make it personal** Write a short paragraph comparing yourself to a friend or relative.

Can you remember ...
- 10 parts of the body? SB→p.124
- 8 parts of the face? SB→p.125
- 12 description words or phrases? SB→p.125
- 9 adjectives? SB→p.126
- 16 personality adjectives? SB→p.128
- 9 geographical features? SB→p.130

Audio Script

Unit 1

▶ 1.1
Countries
Australia – Australian
Brazil – Brazilian
Canada – Canadian
Chile – Chilean
India – Indian
Korea – Korean
Continents
Africa – African
America – American
Asia – Asian
Europe – European

▶ 1.3
HBO
CNN
ABC
BBC
MTV
VH1
ESPN
NBC

▶ 1.6
1 The total is thirty euros.
2 Here's your ticket and twenty-five dollars.
3 That's two dollars. There you go. Enjoy!
4 That's forty-eight dollars! That's ridiculous!

▶ 1.7
C = Cynthia   G = Geoffrey

C Hello, tourist information, this is Cynthia. What can I do for you today?
G Yes, can you help me, please?
C Sure, no problem. I just need some information from you. What's your name?
G Geoffrey Jenkins. That's G-E-O-double-F-R-E-Y. Jenkins, J-E-N-K-I-N-S.
C Thank you. And what is your nationality?
G I'm American
C And what's your hotel address, Mr. Jenkins?
G Hotel Panorama. 63 Sea Parade.
C Thank you. And what's your telephone number?
G My cell number is 860-4279.
C Thanks. And, uh, what's your email address?
G It's gjenkins90@ncfc.com.
C gjenkins19? One nine?
G No, 90, nine zero.
C Ok, thanks. Now what do you want to know?

▶ 1.11
What's your first name?
What's your last name?
Where are you from?
What's your nationality?
What's your address?
How old are you?

▶ 1.12
a How are you?
b What's new?
c See you later.
d Thank you!
e What's up?
f I don't understand.

Unit 2

▶ 2.2
W = woman   M = man

a W Excuse me. What time is it, please?
  M It's six forty-five.
b M Excuse me. Excuse me. What time is it?
  W Uh ... It's about half past seven.
  M Oh, my train!
c W Psst! Is it time to go home yet?
  M No, it's only four o'clock.
d M What time is it?
  W It's twelve forty-five. Time for lunch!
e M Is it two forty-five yet?
  W No! It's a quarter past three.
  M What? Wow, I'm really late.

▶ 2.5
I = interviewer   D = David

I Hello, please introduce yourself and tell us a bit about your family.
D Ok ... My name is David and I have two siblings, Edward and Sandra. Our parents are Richard and Ann. Hmm ... Edward lives with his wife, Alexandra, and their children, Peter and Camilla.

▶ 2.6
W = woman   M = man   G = girl

a W Hey! There you are! So, how old are you now?
  M Uh ... twenty-one.
  W Haha! You always say that! Here's your gift. Happy birthday!
b M Look! It's eleven fifty-nine ... quick everybody. Get a drink!
  All 10, 9, 8, 7, 6, 5, 4, 3, 2, 1 ... Happy New Year!
  M Happy New Year!
c W Do you have everything?
  G Yes, Mom.
  W Do you have your passport?
  G Yes, Mom.
  W OK, darling. Have a good trip!
  G OK. See you soon.
d All Jingle bells, jingle bells, jingle all the way. Hey! Merry Christmas!
  W Merry Christmas!
e W I love weddings and you look fantastic! Congratulations!
f G Hmmmmm. That smells delicious!
  M Thank you. We have chicken and vegetables to start and then fruit salad. Enjoy your meal.

Unit 3

▶ 3.2
W = woman   M = man   G = girl

a W What is the weather like today?
  G It's really nice. Very warm and sunny, I love it!
b W Is it hot out?
  M Yes, it is. It's 40 degrees! I hate it.
c W1 What is the weather usually like in your city?
  W2 It's usually very windy, but today it's calm.
d M1 How is the weather these days?
  M2 It's cold and rainy. Yuck!
e W Is it snowy in July in your country?
  M Yes, in some places. You need a warm jacket!

Audio Script

3.6

R = Rita   T = Taylor   S = Selena
J = Josh   I = Isobel

R This evening in *Job Corner* we have four different professionals. First let's meet Taylor Gregor. Hi, Taylor.
T Hi, Rita.
R So tell us, Taylor, what do you do?
T I'm a web designer.
R Tell us about your routine. Do you have to get up early every morning?
T No, I don't have to get up early at all. I make my own hours.
S Well, my name is Serena James, and I'm a police officer.
R Do you have a fixed schedule?
S Yes, I have to be at the station at six thirty every morning. Sometimes I need to work weekends, too.
R I see. I want to ask Josh and Isobel the same question. Please tell our listeners what you do.
J Well, we are Josh and Isobel Markham and we work together.
R What do you do?
I Josh and I are singers. We sing at nightclubs.
R So you have free mornings and afternoons?
J No, we don't. We have to work in the afternoon to prepare for the evening presentation.
R Are you all happy with your jobs?
J/I Yeah, sure, yes.
T I think so, yes. I have a lot of freedom and I use my creativity every day.
R How about you, Serena?
S To be honest, I want to change jobs. The work in the police force is very hard, and I want to get married and have kids. So I want to go back to college and become a teacher. They have long vacations.
R OK, it's time for our break. More from our guests after these messages …

3.7

P = Philip   S = Sarah

P Mom! I feel bad. My stomach and, and my head.
S Oh, baby! What's the matter? Are you OK?
P No, Mom. I'm not. I feel really bad. I feel …
S What is it? Do you have a fever? Are you hot?
P Oh, yes, yes. And then sometimes I'm very cold.
S Oh, baby! Are you hungry?
P No, no. I'm not hungry. But I'm very thirsty. And I feel tired.

Unit 4

4.1

R = Rob   C = Claire

R Claire, what time does Randy have soccer practice today?
C Oh, Rob! He only has soccer practice on Monday. Today is Tuesday.
R Oh, right, sorry. So today Chloe has her …
C Swimming class. Yes, at four thirty.
R So what is Randy doing today?
C Rob, please! Look at the schedule! He has soccer on Monday and tennis practice on Thursday. Chloe swims on Tuesday and has ballet classes on Friday afternoon. What kind of father are you?
R The kind that has a terrible memory?
C Well, Chloe finishes at six thirty today. Don't forget that! And you have to take them both to volleyball on Saturday.

4.7

K = Katie   B = Brian
S1 = salesperson 1   S2 = salesperson 2

K Oh, Brian! Can we go in here?
B Oh, Katie! Not again! How many stores do we have to go to?
K Oh, come on, Brian. This is the last one. I promise.
B Come on then, let's go.
K Great!

K Hey, Brian, what do you think of this blouse?
B It's … uh … It's interesting.
K Look, Brian. I need to do some shopping and you are not helping. You need some new jeans. Why don't you go and try some on? See you later.
B Fine. See you later.

S1 Hi. Do you need any help?
B Yes, I, uh … can I try those jeans on, please?
S1 Sure. What size?
B Uh … medium … I think.
S1 Medium? Here you are. The fitting rooms are over there.
B Thank you.

B Uh … excuse me … can I get these in a large, please?
S1 Of course, sir. Here you are.

B Hi, Katie. So, these are my new jeans. What do you think?
K They look great, Brian. Really good.
B What are you getting?
K Well, I have these shorts and uh … this blouse.
B Oh. The … blouse.
K What?
B Well … it's just … it's the color. Orange and … and pink … and …
S2 Next, please! Hello, ma'am. Shorts and a blouse. That's …
K No, no. Not the blouse. Er … Only the shorts, please.
S2 OK. That's $60, please.
K How much? Uh … I … No. No, thank you. Come on, Brian, let's go.

Unit 5

5.4

B = Becky   L = Leo

B Hey, Leo. Look at these statistics! They are crazy!
L I don't know, Becky. Only one hour a day playing video games. I love video games. I play for two hours a day easily.
B Really! Ugh, video games! I hate them. They are so boring!
L OK, well, what about you? What do you like doing?
B Well, I like going out with friends, you know, socializing. Not just sitting at home playing video games all the time.
L Hey! I like to go out, too! I just don't like shopping. That's what you do all the time.
B Ugh! No way! I don't like shopping either. I don't mind shopping malls, because I love to watch movies …

55

Audio Script

L Ha! So you love to sit in the movie theater watching movies and I love to sit in my room playing video games.

▶ 5.5

I = interviewer   C = Celia

I So, Celia, tell me about Angelo. Does he help you around the house?
C Well, he's not too bad, I mean, he doesn't mind doing his laundry—not the laundry, just his. But he absolutely hates washing the dishes and he never cleans his room—it's chaos in there!
I And what does he do in his free time?
C Oh, he's in his bedroom a lot. He loves playing video games and watching movies. All the time.
I What about you? Do you like doing the chores?
C No, I don't! I guess Angelo is like me! Hmm ... I guess I don't mind washing the dishes because I know I can do it correctly. I hate cleaning the bathroom, but I have to do it.
I And how about your free time?
C Free time! You're joking! Hmm ... I love to swim when I can, and I like to read novels, too. But I don't really have time for anything like that.

▶ 5.6

a You can snorkel, kayak or swim.
b No, you don't. There are many ways to explore them.
c No, they don't. They live on land, in the forests.
d The five examples of wildlife are penguins, turtles, flamingoes, sea lions, and tortoises.

▶ 5.7

B = Beth

B: Hi, everyone! Here I am in the beautiful city of Bath. I've got a new job for the summer – I'm a house sitter. The family are in New York on holiday and I'm taking care of their house, garden, two dogs, one cat, and lots of fish!
It's a big house with a garden, and I have a list of chores I have to do every day. Most of them are fun and I don't mind doing them, but I don't like watering the plants. They have lots and lots of plants!! It's very hot here this summer, so every morning I open the windows and doors and let the cat out. He usually sleeps under a tree all day. Then I feed the dogs, Toby and Freddie, and give the fish some food – they have 8 beautiful fish. I check there is some clean water for the cat, and after breakfast I take the dogs for a long walk. They love going to the park and swimming in the lake there.
When I get home, I pick up the mail and put it on the table in the kitchen I spend most of the day reading or sunbathing in the garden. Sometimes I go sightseeing in Bath. It's brilliant! In the evening I close the windows, wash the dishes, and go to bed.
I don't get paid for this job, but I love being a house sitter.

▶ 5.8

a Hi, Martin, can you water the plants and feed the cat? Oh, and please don't close the windows. Don't worry, the cat can't escape, she's too fat.
b Hi, Tim, I'm working late today. Please cook dinner and prepare a salad. Don't wash the dishes. I can do them after dinner. Bye for now.
c Hi, it's me again. Don't walk the dog, he has a bad foot. But don't forget to feed him. See you later.
d Hi, darling. There's no herbal tea in the kitchen. Can you go to the grocery store and buy some, please? Love you.

▶ 5.10

M = man   W = woman   G = girl
B = boy

a M Is there a museum near here?
  W Yes, it's about five minutes from here. Go straight along Station Road and turn left on Drury Street, it's on your right. It's very big, you can't miss it.
  M Thanks.
b G Is there a bookstore near here?
  M Yeah, it's there, on the corner of Station Road and Holt Street.
  G Oh, yes, thank you.
c B Do you know where the ID English school is?
  W Hmm ... I think you have to turn right on Holt Street and then right again after the library. The school is on that street.
d M1 Are there any clubs in this town?
  M2 Yeah, there's one near Luigi's. Go straight on Station Road and take the second right. Then turn left on Ruddy Street. The club is on the left, opposite the restaurant.
e W Where is a good place to exercise here?
  M There is a gym near the mall. Go to the end of Holt Street and turn left on Pilkington Road. The gym is the first building on your right.

Unit 6

▶ 6.1

M = Mom   H = Hannah

M Hannah?
H Yes, Mom?
M Could you go to the store for me? The refrigerator is empty.
H Uh, I guess. Do you have a list?
M Not really, but we can write one really quickly.
H OK, so what do we need?
M Some milk and, uh, six eggs.
H OK. Oh, and we need some tea, too. I used the last bag last night.
M Hmm, do you want some fish for dinner?
H Sure.
M So get a pound of fish, too. Oh, and three onions and four potatoes to cook the fish with.
H Yummy.
M Yes. Anything else you want?
H We don't have any fruit. Can I get some apples and oranges?
M Yes, and some bananas, too. I like to eat them for breakfast.
H I know. So, is that it?
M Read it to me.
H Milk, six eggs, tea, fish, three onions, four potatoes, apples, oranges, and bananas. Is it OK if I get some chocolate as well?
M Just a small bar for you.
H OK! Then off to the grocery store I go. Call me if you remember something else.
M I will. Thanks, hon.

Audio Script

Unit 7

7.2

P = presenter   J = Jude

P Hello and welcome to another episode of Project Renovation, the program where we visit people on the project of a lifetime as they rebuild, restore, and renovate old houses. Today we're in Springfield, where Phillip and Jude are working on their house. Jude, what are you doing today?
J Hi. Well, today we are working on the bathroom. Uh … In the original plans there was no bathroom, or toilet, so this is a big part of the project.
P What? No bathroom! No toilet! That's unbelievable!
J Well, there was a bathtub next to the fireplace in the living room and the … uh … the toilet was in the yard. Well, obviously, we want a toilet and a bathroom in the house, so Phillip is making a new bathroom above the utility room.
P I see, and are there any other big differences?
J Oh, yes, of course. In the original plans there was a kitchen and a dining room, but they were both very, very small. Oh, and there were no windows in the kitchen, so it was very dark. Uh … now we have one big room—the kitchen and the dining room are together—and new windows, so there is a lot of light.
P That's great. So now you can cook here and …
J Well, no, we can't cook here yet. There's no stove and no refrigerator, they are coming next week, I hope! Uh, at the moment we are using the microwave and eating a lot of pizza.
P Hmm … healthy. So what do you like most about this house?
J Well, I know that Phillip is very excited about his new office. And I really love the yard. There's space for children to run and play, when we start a family, of course.
P Great. Well, thank you for talking to us, Jude. I'll visit again when you finish the house. Bye.
J Yes, please do! Thanks for coming. Bye!

7.4

A Wow, you look tired. What were you doing over the weekend?
B Yeah, I am tired. I was at Mari's party on Saturday until really late.
A Oh, gee! Was it a good party?
B Yeah, it was great! It was on the beach and I was there until the morning.
A Really? You were there all night? Weren't you cold?
B No, no, the night was warm, so it was ok.
A That's cool!
B Yeah, it was great. There were fireworks at midnight and a lot of pizza for the guests. Mari doesn't like cake, can you believe it?
A What? No cake? At a birthday party? I can't believe it! Well, was it a big party?
B Hmm, there were about 30 people at the beginning, but there were only five on Sunday morning! It was a great night, but I am feeling it today! And I have to work!
A Oh, well, drink a lot of coffee!

7.8

The organizers sold all the tickets in 30 minutes. The tickets were $228 each. The festival is 5 days, but there's music on only 3 days.
There were 60 stages.
There were 1,300 recycling volunteers.
There were over 2,200 performances.
There were 5,489 toilets, and there were 300 people cleaning them.
There were over 220,000 people in the audience.

7.9

M = man   W = woman   B = boy
G = girl

a M1 Would you like to go to a soccer game?
   M2 Sure, that sounds great. When is it?
   M1 Saturday afternoon.
   M2 Saturday? Oh, no! I have to work on Saturday. Sorry.
b M Do you want to go to the movies this weekend?
   W Uh. I'm free on Saturday night. Is that good for you?
   M Yes. See you Saturday then.
c W1 Would you like to come to a party on Saturday?
   W2 I'd love to. What can I bring?
   W1 Nothing. Just yourself.
d B How about going to the park after lunch?
   G Good idea. Let's go.
e M I'm having a barbecue on Friday. Can you make it?
   W Friday? I'm sorry. I'm going to a party. Maybe next time.
f M We're going to a restaurant for our 25th wedding anniversary. Can you come?
   W Oh, congratulations! Of course I can come. I'd love to!

Unit 8

8.8

A = Alyssa   G = Ginny

A Welcome to Celebrity Present and Past. I'm Alyssa Meyers. Today in our studio we're interviewing pop singer Ginny Lomond. Ginny, thank you for being here today.
G Hi, Alyssa.
A Our viewers are so curious about your life. So, when did you start your career?
G At the age of 12, actually. I was part of my school glee club.
A Really? And where did you go to school?
G I went to school here, in New York City.
A Oh, so are you originally from New York?
G No, I was born in Los Angeles, but my mother and I moved to New York when I was a baby.
A When did you record your first album?
G When I was 18, but it was a disaster!
A No, that's not possible!
G But it was! Then I recorded my second album in 2008. And I have to say, that one was a big success!
A We know it was. Well, our lines are open. If you have a question for Ginny Lomond, call now. She'll answer the questions after the break.

57

Audio Script

8.9

Yesterday Jake woke up at around 6:30 a.m., but he didn't get up immediately. He stayed in bed for three or four minutes, then he got up and made his bed. Then he exercised for 30 minutes. After that, he took a shower, shaved, got dressed, and had breakfast: coffee, juice, and cereal. Then he brushed his teeth and, finally, left home at around 8 a.m.

8.11

W = woman   M = man   B = boy
G = girl

a W1 Could you open the window, please?
   W2 Of course. Are you hot?
b M   Could you please pass me the salt?
   W   Here you are.
c M1 Could you hold the door, please?
   M2 OK.
d M   Could you please lend me your phone?
   W   I'm sorry. I don't have it with me.
e W1 Could you help me, please?
   W2 Sure. What is it?
f W   Could I use your bathroom, please?
   M   Yes, it's the second door on the left.
g B   Could I borrow your pen, please?
   G   Sure. There you go.
h W   Could I have the menu, please?
   M   Of course, madam. Just a minute.
i M   Could I speak to Mr. Green, please?
   W   Who's speaking, please?

Unit 9

9.4

W = woman   M = man

a M Excuse me. What do you do?
   W I'm a computer programmer.
b M What's your profession?
   W I'm a dentist.
c W Are you an engineer?
   M No, I'm a photographer.
d W What's your job?
   M I'm a personal assistant. I work in an office.
e M Are you a student?
   W No, I'm a flight attendant.
f M Is your job dangerous?
   W Yes, sometimes. I'm a firefighter.
g W That's a smart uniform! Are you a police officer?
   M Yes, I am.

9.7

W = woman   M = man

a W1 Did you make a resolution this year?
   W2 Yes. I'm going to get in shape and exercise more, so next week I'm joining a gym. Or maybe in two weeks.
b M   What's your New Year's resolution?
   W   I'm going to save money. I'm not going to buy unnecessary clothes. I have so many shoes anyway.
c M1 Do you have a resolution this year?
   M2 Yes. I'm going to be more organized. First, I'm going to write a list. Number one ... Hm?
d W1 What's your New Year's resolution?
   W2 I'm going to volunteer. My friend and I are helping at a homeless charity next week.
e W   What do you want to change this year?
   M   Well, I'm going to eat better. I'm taking cooking classes in the evening.
f W   What are you going to change this year?
   M   I'm going to try and relax more. I'm going to go on vacation next month.

9.11

W = woman   M = man   B = boy
G = girl

a B   Dad, could I borrow the car tonight?
   M   Uh ... where are you going?
   B   Oh, only to Joe's house. We need to ... hmm ... work on our school project.
   M   Sure, go ahead. But drive slowly!
b M1 Can I ask you a question?
   M2 Yeah. Go ahead.
   M1 Do you make a lot of money?
   M2 I'm sorry, but I don't like to talk about money.
c W1 Could you lend me some money for the drink machine?
   W2 No problem. Here you are.
d W   Is it OK if I turn off the air conditioning?
   M   Oh, are you cold?
   W   Yes! Really cold!
   M   Oh, sorry. Go ahead.
e B   Do you mind if I sit here?
   G   I'm sorry, but my friend is sitting here.
f W1 Do you mind if I take your photo?
   W2 Not at all. Cheese!

Unit 10

10.1

This is Amy. She's about 45 and has fair hair. She's Jay's daughter. And this person is Carmen. She is from Colombia. She is slim and young and she has long dark hair. Next to her you can see Jay. He is married to Carmen. Jay is old and he has short gray hair. On the other side of the picture you can see Joseph and Cameron. Joseph is Jay's son. He is average height and average build. Cameron is Joseph's partner. She is tall and overweight.

10.3

This is a picture of my soccer team. So, the player at the front, the slim one, that's Michael. He's slim and he's very fast! And the player next to him is Lewis. We call him the Mad Scientist because he looks like Albert Einstein. But he's clever, he's more intelligent than the other players. Uh... Who else? Oh, yes! This is Wayne, he's more overweight than the other players, but he's still a good player! And this one's Frank. He's happier than all the others. Frank's always happy, even when we lose.
And this is Phil, he's only 17. He's younger than the rest of the team. Then, at the back you can also see Peter. He's so tall, over two meters! He's taller than everyone else in the team. And there's Steve, too. He's stronger than the other players and he's not very friendly. And this one is little Rory. He's shorter than everyone, but he's a very good player!

Audio Script

10.5

a perfectionist, spontaneous, disorganized
b angry, moody, loyal
c possessive, romantic, suspicious
d idealistic
e arrogant, negative, positive

10.6

W = woman   M = man   G = girl
B = boy

a W Excuse me. I need to get to the city center. Where's the nearest subway station?
  M It's a couple of blocks from here. Just keep going straight. It's in the shopping mall.
b G Wow, there are so many trees here. Is this the biggest park in the city?
  W No, the biggest one is Green Park. It's next to the river.
c B What's the most important thing in the museum?
  W We have some Egyptian artifacts on the second floor. They are very rare.
d M So, let's go dancing tonight. What's the best nightclub in the city?
  W Sorry? What did you say?
  M The best nightclub.
  W Oh. That's *Venom*. It's behind the movie theater.
  M Ok, let's go!
e G Which is your cheapest can of soda?
  M It's this one.
  G OK. I'll take one of those.
  M That's two dollars, please.

10.9

T = Tess   M = Mary

T Hi, Mary, where were you last week? You weren't at work.
M Oh, Tess, didn't I tell you? I was on vacation.
T Awesome. How was it?
M It was beautiful! I went swimming in the ocean and did some sunbathing on the beach and I went walking in the mountains. There were lots of lizards sitting on the rocks in the sun, they were so cute! I enjoyed it a lot.
T Lizards! Ugh! I hate them. But the ocean sounds nice. Was it hot?
M Oh, the weather was perfect, it only rained once. How about you? Are you going on vacation this year?
T Yes, I am. I'm going to Indonesia next month. I'm really excited!
M I can imagine. Everyone says Indonesia is amazing.

10.11

M1 = man 1   M2 = man 2

M1 Do you like wrestling?
M2 Yeah, it's great! Are you going to watch the fight next weekend? David Silver against Danny Belching.
M1 Of course! Who do you think is going to win?
M2 That's a difficult question. I think maybe Danny Belching. He is stronger and he has a lot of energy, he doesn't get tired.
M1 That's true, but David Silver is taller and his arms are longer. I think his technique is better, too. I think he's going to win.
M2 It's true that he is taller, but Danny is a little faster. And remember, Danny won his last two fights, but David lost his. I think it's going to be Danny's night.
M1 Hmm, maybe you're right. Let's wait and see.

Answer Key

Unit 1

1.1
1 **Countries**
Australia, Brazil, Canada, Chile, India, Korea
Continents
Africa, America, Asia, Europe
2 Australian, Brazilian, Canadian, Chilean, Indian, Korean, African, American, Asian, European
3 b Indian c Chinese d Korea e Peruvian
4 1 B 's / Austra**lian**
  2 A **Are**   B **'m not** / Korean
  3 A **Is** / Peruvian B Indian / **'s**
  4 A American   B **they're not** / **'re British**
  5 A Me**xican**   B **isn't** / **'s** / Spanish
5 b ✓
  c My brother is **a** horrible singer.
  d You are **an** excellent actor.
  e ✓
  f ✓
6 a I think *Star Wars* is a terrible movie.
  b Luis Suárez is an excellent player.
  c I think São Paulo is a great city.
  d I think India is an interesting country.
  e Chris Pratt is a cool actor.
7 Personal answers.

1.2
1 a HBO b CNN c ABC d BBC e MTV f VH1 g ESPN h NBC
2 b go c a name d ten e eight f six g one
3 f hi – five
  c a guitar – a party
  g no – a nose
  b blue – you
  a a name – Spain
  e ten – yes
4 one, two, three, four, five, six, seven, eight, nine, ten
5 1 $16 / $14 2 $75 / $100 3 $20 / $10 4 $12 / $4
6 1 30 2 25 3 2 4 48
7 Hi! Nice **to meet** you. My first name's _____ and my last name's _____. I'm _____.
I'm from _____. I'm _____.

1.3
1 First name: **Geoffrey**
  Last name: **Jenkins**
  Hotel address: Hotel **Panorama**, 63 Sea Parade.
  Phone: **860-4279**
  Email: **gjenkins90@nfc.com**
3 a What's your (full) name?
  b Where do you live?
  c What's your cell phone / phone number?
  d What's your address?
  e What's your email address?
4 Personal answers.
5 laptop, key, sandwich, glasses, phone, lipstick
6

+ S	+ ES	–Y + IES
backpacks	addresses	cities
earrings	glasses	countries
keys	sandwiches	nationalities
phones		

7 1 This 2 That 3 These / them 4 those / They 5 These / They

1.4
1 our, his, your, their
2 a ~~her~~ his b ~~her~~ your c ~~his~~ her d ~~ours~~ our e ~~they're~~ their f ~~yours~~ your
3 a The White House b The Pink House c Shakira d Levi's e Snoopy f Purple g Red and yellow h Nemo
  i An apple j Charlie Brown k "Where is the love?"

1.5
1 1 American 2 Jamaica 3 08/31/90 4 Patel 5 23 6 45 Colt Street, Dallas, Texas
2 Personal answers.
3 a 1 Fine, thanks. b 2 Not much.
  c 1 Bye, for now. d 2 You're welcome.
  e 2 Nothing much. f 1 Oh, sorry.
4 Personal answers.

Unit 2

2.1
1 a to b to the c to the d to a / the /to e - f to g to
3 a Sunday b Wednesday c Friday d Monday e Tuesday f Thursday g Saturday
4 a 4 b Saturn c Friday
5 b 7:30 c 4:00 d 12:45 e 3:15
6 a It's six fifteen b It's half past six.
  c It's five o'clock. d It's twelve fifteen.
  e It's two forty-five.
7 a What time do you go to school? b What time do you go to bed? c What time do you go to work? d What time do you get home? e What time do you get up? f What time do you go to the gym?
8 Personal answers.

2.2
1 b get dressed / up c get up / dressed d have breakfast e leave home f make the bed g take a shower h wake up
2 Personal answers.
3 at six thirty, immediately, for around, for twenty minutes, at around
4 a F b T c T d T e F f T
5 Personal answers.
6 A love B loves C loves D don't love E love F love / love / loves G love H doesn't love

2.3
1 David's family tree
  a Richard   e Alexandra
  b Ann   f Camilla
  c Sandra   g Peter
  d Edward
2 a F b T c T d F e F f F g T h F i T j T
3 a brother b wife c father d sister e grandfather f son g niece h grandson
4 a What is your full name? b Where are you from? c Where do you live? d Do you like this city? e Do you have a big family?
5 Personal answers.
6 (Possible answers)
  a What's her name?
  b Where does she / your sister live?
  c Does she like Bogotá?
  d Who is that old man?
  e Is he Chinese?

2.4
1 b often c occasionally d sometimes e always f often g never
2 Personal answers.
3 Personal answers.

2.5
1 b Where **do** you live? c **Do** you have a boyfriend / girlfriend? d What time **do** you go to bed on weekdays? e Do you **have** any brothers or sisters? f Do **you** use the Internet? g What **do** you do on the weekend?
2 Personal answers.
3 1 What is his / her name? 2 When is your birthday? 3 How often do you use it? 4 How many hours do you sleep? 5 What do you do on weekdays? 6 Is it a cool city? 7 How old are they?
4 a 2 b 6 c 1 d 4 e 7 f 3 g 5
5 1 **always** 6 **never** 5 occasionally 3 often 4 sometimes 2 usually
6 Personal answers.
7 a **Happy birthday!**   d **Merry Christmas!**
  b **Happy New Year!**   e **Congratulations!**
  c **Have a good trip!** f **Enjoy your meal!**

Unit 3

3.1
1 b rain c wind d cloud e sun f snow, snow, snow
  Pictures: 1e, 2d, 3a, 4f, 5b, 6c
3 b in c does d in e the
4 c, e, a, d, b
5 a sunny, cold, warm, rainy b rainy, hot, sunny c snowing, cold d cloudy, sun e fog, foggy

3.2
1 islands, the Caribbean, the capital, northwest, big, January, June, July, December, February, March
2 a T b F c T d T e F f F
3 is starting, is getting, are becoming, is doing, is buying, am writing
4 1 Are you busy / Call you later 2 I can't hear you / No problem 3 Sorry, wrong number 4 The line's busy

3.3
1 1 c 2 d 3 f 4 a 5 b 6 e
2 a Is your mum sleeping? No, she's working.
  b What are you doing in the kitchen? I'm making cookies.
  c Where is he living these days? He's living in Mexico City.
  d Who is your brother dancing with? He's dancing with his girlfriend.
  e Are they playing tennis? No, they're playing basketball.
  f What are you drinking now? I'm drinking a cup of coffee.
3 (Possible answers)
  2 He's cooking. / He's making lunch.
  3 She's drinking a cup of coffee.
  4 He's riding a motorcycle.
  5 They're watching TV.
  6 He's eating breakfast.
4 a isolation b violence c consumerism d identity theft e Internet addiction

3.4
1 a He's an athlete. Now he's driving (a/his car).
  b This is Emma Watson. She's an actor. Now she's eating.
  c This is Drake. He's a singer. Now he's watching basketball.
  d This is Malala Yousafzai. She's an activist. Now she's reading.
2 Personal answers.
3 1 are you doing, drinking a coffee, relaxing, do you do, have a coffee
  2 are you riding, am riding, ride
  3 are you reading, don't, read, read, like
  4 are watching, are watching, watch,
4 are, jump, use, are planning, want, need, is checking

Answer Key

3.5

1. want to, have to, want to, have to, have to, want to, have to

2.

	want to +	want to −	have to +	have to −
Taylor				a
Josh and Isobel			d	
Serena	e, f		b, c	

3. a He's a web designer. b She's a police officer. c They are singers. d She wants to be a teacher.
4. Personal answers.
5. hot, cold, thirsty, tired
6. a Do you want a cold drink? ✓
   b Would you want a hot drink? ✓
   c Do you want a sweater? ✓
   d Would you like to stay at home today? ✓
   e Do you want to go out? ✗
   f Would you like a sandwich? ✗
   g Do you want to go to hospital? ✓

Unit 4

4.1

1. a volleyball b basketball c golf d baseball e soccer f American football g tennis h rugby
2. a Golf. It isn't a team game.
   b Volleyball. You use your hands to hit the ball.
   c Cycling. You don't do it in water.
   d Soccer. You have to score points.
   e Skiing. You can only do it in winter.
3. Chloe: swimming on Tuesday, ballet on Friday, volleyball on Saturday
   Randy: soccer on Monday, tennis on Thursday, volleyball on Saturday
4. a Chloe b 4.30 c 6.30 d Rob (dad)
5. Personal answers.

4.2

1. Play: the drums, soccer, the piano
   Drive: a bus, a car, a tractor
   Speak: Chinese, French, Korean
   Cook: Indian food, pasta, a special meal
2. c, a, d, b
3. a Tennis and swimming are good for training.
   b No, he sings songs by Bob Marley and Otis Redding.
   c His partner, Lisa.
   d He speaks four languages.
   e He likes learning languages and they are useful for his profession.
   f He thinks it's a beautiful game.
4. Personal answers.

4.3

1. a can, can b can c can't d can't e Can't, can't, can't f Can't g can h Can
2. b Can Chloe cook? No, she can't.
   c Can Maria drive a car? Yes, she can.
   d Can Kyle play the violin? No, he can't.
   e Can Sam swim? Yes, he can.
   f Can Amy ski? No, she can't.
4. Personal answers.

4.4

1. a Jeans and a T-shirt. b One. c No, some are wearing just socks. d No, only two. e The first man from the right. f The young girl. g No, two are wearing T-shirts. h Only one. The third woman from the right. i None.
2. Personal answers.
3. a shoes b sandals / boots c dress d blouse / skirt e shirt
4. a A dress and some shoes. b Favorite. c A shirt and a skirt. d $75 e Personal answers.

5. Mine, yours, ours, theirs, 's, hers, His, Whose
7. Personal answers.

4.5

1. d, a, c, e, b
2. S Hi, can I help you?
   J Hello, can I try on those shorts in **the store window**?
   S Sure, here you are. **The fitting rooms** are over there.
   J They are great! Can I pay by **credit card**?
   S Of course. Is it **contactless**?
   J Yes it is. Can I have a **receipt**, please?
4. a No, he doesn't. b A clothes store. c L. d $60 e Nothing.
6. Personal answers.

Unit 5

5.1

1. **Across:** 1 movie theater 3 river 8 bookstore 9 club
   Down: 2 swimming pool 3 racetrack 4 park 5 mall 6 hotel 7 library
2. a● b● c○● d○●● e● f●○○ g●○○ h●○
3. Personal answers.
4. a There's a museum downtown. b There are no movie theaters here. c There aren't any big parks. d There are some good restaurants. e There's a fantastic bookstore. f There are two small rivers.
5. a there's b there's c There's d There are e There's f Is there g Is there h there are i Are there

5.2

1. a cleaning the house b shopping c cooking d eating out e exercising f going out g watching TV h playing video games
2. They both like going out.
4. a Clean the bathroom. b Play video games. c Wash the dishes. d Watch a movie. e Do the laundry. f Tidy the bedroom.
5. a A newspaper b giving information
6. a doesn't mind b hates c cleans d loves e doesn't like f doesn't mind g hates h doesn't have i loves j likes

5.3

1. Photo 1 shows the islands. Photo 2 shows a giant tortoise. Photo 3 shows sea turtles on sand.
2. a You can snorkel, kayak, or swim.
   b No, you don't. There are many ways to explore them.
   c No, they don't. They live on land, in the forests.
   d Penguins, turtles, flamingoes, sea lions, tortoises.
3. Katy: visiting museums, sightseeing, eating out
   Sara: snorkeling, camping, kayaking
   Tom: sunbathing, reading novels, swimming
4. reading novels, sightseeing, kayaking, snorkeling, sunbathing, swimming, taking a class, shopping

5.4

1. taking, watering, open, let, feed, give, check, take, pick, put, close, wash
2. a She's living in Bath.
   b He likes sleeping under a tree (all day).
   c She doesn't get any money. / None.
3. a ✓/✓/✗ b ✓/✓/✗ c ✗/✓/✗ d ✓/✗/✓
4. a Open / them / night b her c don't / dishes / them d him e it

5.5

1. a safe b cheap c messy d boring e near
2. a F b T c T d F
3. 1 d 2 c 3 a 4 b

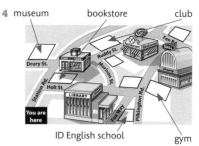

4 museum bookstore club ID English school gym

7. Personal answers.

Unit 6

6.1

1. a chocolate b fish c lettuce d spaghetti e oranges f tomatoes g vinegar h potatoes i chicken j sugar
   Sentence: We went to the grocery store and bought lots of things.
2. Some milk, six eggs, some tea, some fish, three onions, four potatoes, apples, oranges, bananas, chocolate.
3. a the last bag
   b fish / dinner
   c fish / onions / potatoes
   d bananas / breakfast
   e chocolate
4. Personal answers.
5.

Countable	Uncountable
carrot	tea / coffee
onion	milk
egg	bread
banana	butter
grape	cheese
orange	oil
apple	rice
kiwi	

6.2

1. a a can b a cup c a piece d a slice e a bowl f a glass g a bottle
2. some, any, a, a, any, some, some, any, an, any
3. a coffee with milk, bread and butter
   b sometimes c vegetables d orange juice e chocolate f every day
4. Personal answers.

6.3

1. a little, a little, a few, a few, a little, a little
2. a healthy diet b fast food c (a little) fruit d a lot of
3. (Second column sequence) b, d, c, e, a
4. a a little b a little c a few d a little e a few
5. Personal answers.

6.4

1. a F b F c F d T e T
2. 1 Do you have a healthy diet?
   2 how much fruit do you eat every day?
   3 how many bananas do you eat every week?
   4 Do you like all vegetables?
   5 How many vegetables do you usually eat every week?
   6 How much meat do you eat?
   7 How much fast food do you eat?
   8 How many cups of tea or coffee do you drink every day?
   9 Do you eat anything unhealthy?
   10 how many slices of chocolate cake do you eat every week?
3. meat, onion, tomatoes, tomato, oil, salt

61

Answer Key

4 How much, a little, a few, How many, how much, a few, How many, a lot, How much, a little

6.5
1 **Down:** 1 grapes 3 steak 4 spinach
  Across: 2 pepper 3 salmon 5 pie 6 onions
  7 strawberries
2 **Courses:** starters, main courses, desserts
  How it's cooked: pureed, grilled, barbecued, sautéed, steamed, baked
  Fruits: lemon, melon, pears
  Vegetables: lettuce, carrots, onions
3 Would you, don't, Would you, like, would you, wouldn't, liked
4 Can I have the menu, Would you like to order a starter, I'll have the chicken salad, Anything to drink, I would like a diet soda, Could you bring me a clean plate

Unit 7

7.1
1 **Odd word**   **Room**
   b fireplace   bathroom
   c armchair   kitchen
   d oven   office
   e bathtub   bedroom
   f bed   living room
   g fan   garage
   h shower   dining room
   i TV   laundry room
2 a bedroom b living room c kitchen d basement
  e laundry room f office g garage h bathroom
  i dining room
4 Personal answers.
5 a T b F c F
6 a was no b was c wasn't d were no / weren't any
7 a bathroom b utility room c dining room
  d stove e microwave f office

7.2
1 b balloons c cake / candles d snacks
  e lemonade / cola f coffee / tea g plates / napkins g glasses h fireworks i music
2 Personal answers.
3 b How was **it**? c Where **was** it? d What **was** the weather like? e **Was** there a lot of food? f **Were** there fireworks? g **Was** there a cake? h How many people **were** there at the party?
5 a On Saturday. b Great. c On the beach.
  d Warm. e Yes, there was pizza. f Yes, there were. g No, there wasn't. h About 30.
6 Personal answers.
7 h, c, a, g, e, b, d, i, f

7.3
1 a New Year's Eve in Rio
  b Mardi Gras
  c Tomatina
2 **Julianne** was, were
  Lucas was, were, was
3 across from, Next to, above, in front of, under, on, Behind, In
4 Personal answers.

7.4
1 1 a 2016 b 1903 c 1990 d 2012 e 1912 f 1972
2 1988
  was, wasn't, was, were, wasn't, weren't, was
  Today
  are, isn't, is, are, isn't, is, aren't, is, are, isn't
3 Personal answers.

7.5
1 a In the southwest of England.
  b In the summer, at the end of June.
  c A music and arts festival.
  d You have to register online at www.glastonburyfestivals.co.uk.
2 5 days
  60 stages
  1,300 recycling volunteers
  Over 2,200 performances
  5,489 toilets
  220,000 people in the audience
3 The tickets were $228 each.
  There are only 3 days of music.
  300 people cleaning the toilets.
4 a *to go* / soccer game
  b *want* / the movies
  c *Would* / a party
  d *going* / the park
  e a barbecue / *make*
  f a restaurant / *come*

Unit 8

8.1
1 a married b learned c agreed d died e wanted
  f started g studied h worked
2 was born, weren't, worked, helped, studied, moved, started, joined, loved, were, played, follow, invented, were, listed, received, loved, was, watched, enjoyed, married, had, followed, died
3 a T b F c F d N e T f F
5 a Whitney Houston was born on August 9, 1963 in Newark, New Jersey.
  b She recorded her first album in 1985.
  c She received her first Grammy in 1986.
  d She (got) married (to) Bobby Brown in July 18, 1992.
  e She starred in the movie *The Bodyguard* in 1992.
  f She produced the movie *Sparks* in September 2011.
  g She died in a hotel in February 9, 2012.

8.2
1 1 finished / wanted / sailed / helped / stayed
  2 decided / arrived
  3 studied / cried
  4 took / left / gave / saw / flew / got / made / said / had
2 1 played / started
  2 invited / used
  3 tried
  4 bought / came / did / went / knew / thought
3 on, in, at, of, In, in, In, in, In, in, on
4 a second b first c eleventh / twenty-first
  d twenty-third e twentieth

8.3
1 Personal answers.
2 a Who did you go with?
  b Where did you stay?
  c Did you meet anyone?
  d Did you take a lot of photos?
  e What did you buy?
3 b She didn't go to Turkey on vacation. She went on business.
  c She didn't take a plane. She got a ride.
  d The trip didn't take six hours. It took thirteen hours.
  e They didn't stop at a restaurant in Istanbul. They stopped at a restaurant in Ankara.
  f They didn't eat Japanese food. They ate Turkish food.
  g She liked the trip.
5 1 ate 2 made / met 3 said 4 came 5 knew
  6 drank 7 went
6 a Because his girlfriend wanted to go to a different place.
  b No, they went in separate cars.
  c Only $1.
  d Because they were the 1000th client.

8.4
1 1 go to school 2 record first album, record second album 3 move to New York
2 a At the age of 12. b In New York City. c In Los Angeles. d Ginny and her mother moved to New York. e No. f In 2008.
3 a Which magazine elects the 100 most influential people every year?
  b Who did Angelina Jolie divorce in 2016?
  c Who studied fashion design in the 1990s?
  d Who won four Olympic gold medals in tennis?
  e Who did Steven Spielberg meet while filming the second Indiana Jones movie?
  f Where did Ryan Gosling move to in 1996?
4 Yesterday, Jake woke up at around 6:30 a.m., but he didn't get up immediately. He stayed in bed for three or four minutes, then he got up and made his bed. Then he exercised for 30 minutes. After that, he took a shower, shaved, got dressed and had breakfast—coffee, juice and cereal. Then he brushed his teeth and, finally, left home at around 8 a.m.
5 Personal answers.

8.5
1 *The correct form of the verbs are in bold.*
  To Customer Service,
  The delivery **was** late.
  Instead of 3 days, I **had** to wait …
  But then I finally **got** my TV.
  … the sound didn't **work**.
  … but there **was** only noise.
  A person **came** and he **said** the TV …
  … but he didn't **have** it there.
  … but they didn't **know** anything …
  … another repairperson came, **looked** at the TV, **said** that he didn't **have** the necessary part …
  Could you please **help** me?
2 a F b T c T d T e F
3 Personal answers.
4 a open b pass c hold d lend e help f use
  g borrow h have i speak

Unit 9

9.1
1 b a car c a plane d a bus e a truck f a ferry
  g a bike h a train i a motorcycle j on foot
2 a flew b loved c big d hour e ferry
3 1 drove / flew 2 rode 3 took / came
4 1 traffic jam / accident 2 flat tire / late
  3 delayed / wrong turn
5 by foot – **on** foot, by the bus – **by** bus, drove – **rode** her bicycle, flew – **drove** back, walks – **takes** the train, on the cab – **by** cab
6 b How do you usually get to work?
  c Do you take the bus to school?
  d Can you ride a motorcycle?
  e How do you usually get to the supermarket?
  f What's your favorite way to travel?

Answer Key

9.2

1. a It is safe.
   b Two hours.
   c No, there are 2 cables.
   d No. Very young children can use it.
   e No, because not many people live there.
2. (Second column sequence) d, c, e, b, a
3. a computer programmer b dentist
   c photographer d personal assistant
   e flight attendant f firefighter g police officer
4. a What do you do?
   b What's your profession?
   c Are you an engineer?
   d What's your job?
   e Are you a student?
   f Is your job dangerous?
   g Are you a police officer?
5. Personal answers. Suggested answers:
   Computer programmers and dentists make a lot of money. Dangerous jobs are a firefighter and a police officer.

9.3

1. a What time **are** you going to finish work tomorrow?
   b Which team **is** going to win the next World Cup?
   c When are you **going** to go on your next vacation?
   d Where are you going **to** have lunch tomorrow?
   e **Are** you going to do your homework?
   f What are you **going** to do next weekend?
2. 1 going to 2 gonna 3 gonna 4 going to
   5 going to 6 gonna
   a 4 b 6 c 5 d 1 e 3 f 2
3. Personal answers.
4. Picture 1: lightweight, solar-powered cars
   Picture 2: a city roof to protect against rain and snow
   Picture 3: people are going to fold their cars and store them under the bed
5. a T b T c F d F e F

9.4

1. b house c a friend d engaged e a train
   f married
   Losing your keys and moving your bag aren't life changes.
2. a T b T c T d F e F
3. (Second column sequence) c, e, b, f, a, d
4. Next week I'm joining a gym.
   My friend and I are helping at a homeless shelter next week.
   I'm taking cooking classes in the evening.
   I'm going on vacation soon.
   These sentences all have Present Continuous.
6. Personal answers.

9.5

1. c, a, b, e, d
2. Personal answers.
3. (Dialogue order) 3, 7, 4, 1, 5, 6, 2
4. a Could I borrow the **car**, please?
   b Can I ask you a **question**?
   c Could you lend me some **money**?
   d Is it OK if I turn off the **air conditioning**?
   e Do you mind if I **sit** here?
   f Do you mind if I take your **photo**?
6. a ✓ b ✗ c ✓ d ✗ e ✗ f ✓

Unit 10

10.1

1. a mouth b eyes c ears d lips e nose
   Secret question: Do you look like a famous person?
2. a lips / see b eyes / talk c mouth / TV
   d ears / read e nose / movies
3. b chest c fingers d feet e hands f legs
   g stomach h head i arms j teeth
4. a fair hair
   b slim / young / long dark hair
   c old / short gray hair
   d average height / average build
   e tall / overweight

10.2

1. **Similarities:** write stories, tall
   Differences: Nick publishes his stories. Nick has dark hair. Nick's father was athletic.
2. a I am **taller than** my brother.
   b The weather is **worse than** yesterday.
   c My English is **better** than a year **ago**.
   d My sister is **more intelligent than** me.
   e **Children** are **happier** than adults.
   f Dogs are **friendlier than** cats.
   g My grandmother is **more generous than** my mom.
3. **Front, right to left:** Michael, Lewis, Rory, Phil, Wayne, Frank.
   Standing right to left: Peter, Steve.
4. b Lewis is more intelligent than Peter.
   c Michael is slimmer than Steve.
   d Peter is taller than Wayne.
   e Phil is younger than Lewis.
   f Wayne is more overweight than Phil.
   g Steve is stronger than Rory.
   h Frank is happier than Steve.

10.3

1. 1 b 2 e 3 d 4 c 5 a
2. a solitary b idealistic c calm d spontaneous
3. a-f, b-e, c-d
4. a the craziest b the worst c the oldest
   d the biggest e the most popular
   f the most famous g the most difficult
5. a subway station b park c thing d nightclub
   e can
6. a F b T c F d F e T

10.4

1. a is / the / in / the
   b highest / mountain / South
   c The / tallest / in / the / are / the / in
   d are / than
   e is / the / most / in
3. b Madeira / Indonesia c Indonesia d Madeira
   e Madeira / Indonesia f Arizona g Indonesia
   h Arizona
4. a Last week. b Madeira. c Indonesia.
5. a T b T c F d F e F

10.5

1. A Blondes have more hair than people with dark hair.
   B Nerve impulses can travel faster than Formula One cars.
   C Men's hair is thicker than women's hair.
   D A soccer field is bigger than a football field.
   E A dolphin is heavier than an average person.
   F Your hearing is **worse** after you eat.
   G Women have a **stronger** sense of smell than men.
   H Monday is the **most dangerous** day of the week.
   I We are **taller** in the morning.
   J The heart beats **slower** when you sleep.
2. a Next weekend.
   b Danny Belching is stronger and he has a lot of energy, he doesn't get tired. David Silver is taller and his arms are longer.
   c Yes, he did.
3. a stronger b doesn't / tired c taller
   d longer arms e has / better f little faster
   g won / two
4. Personal answers.

Phrase Bank

This Phrase Bank is organized by topics.

Greetings

Unit 1
Nice / Good to meet / see you.
Hello! Nice / Good to meet / see you, too.
How are you (doing)?
How's it going?
What's up?
Fine, thanks.
I'm well, thank you.
Good, thanks.
Things are good / not so good. Not bad.
What about you? / And you?
What's new?
Not much.
Bye for now.
See you later.

Personal information

Unit 1
Are you Peruvian?
Yes, I am. / No, I'm not.
What's your (first) name?
Hi! My name's Maria.
How do you spell your last name / that?
Do you have any brothers and sisters?
I have five brothers and sisters.
What nationality are you?
I'm American. I'm 18 (years old).
I'm 21 (today).
I'm from New York.
Is your mother British?
Yes, she is. / No, she isn't. She's Canadian.
What's your address / phone number / email (address)?
My address is 85 Brown Street.
Where are you from?

Unit 2
How old are you?
Where do you live?
In Madrid, because I work there.
What's your full name?
Do you have a pet?

Your opinion

Unit 1
I think Malala is a very intelligent person.
Yuck! This coffee is horrible.
It's a very cool city.
It's an amazing place.
Yes, I agree.
I think she's ridiculous.
I disagree.

Unit 5
Do you like camping?
I prefer yoga because I enjoy relaxing.
I don't agree. For me ...
I don't like watching TV.
I don't either.
What do you like doing on vacation?
I really like walking.
What about shopping?
We both love it.
In my opinion that's a cheap, fun vacation.
It's an OK place to live.
The most interesting place is probably the racetrack.
I don't mind doing the dishes.
I hate doing the laundry.
I love cell phones, but sometimes ring tones are annoying.

Routine

Unit 2
Do you exercise regularly?
Yes, I do. / No, I don't.
Do you often go to bed late?
How many hours do you sleep?
On average, around seven hours a night.
How often do you go to a café?
Every day after work.
I always have a shower at night before bed.
What time do you get up during the week?
I get up at about six thirty in the morning.
I go to school at seven o'clock from Monday to Friday.
I go to the gym for an hour before / after school.
I have an important meeting on Wednesday.
What do you do on weekends?
When do you go to the grocery store?

Family and relationships

Unit 2
Do you have a girlfriend?
Do you have any brothers or sisters?
No, I'm an only child.
Do you live with your parents?
No, I don't. I live with my girlfriend. / Yes, I do.
How many cousins do you have?
What's your father's name?
Where does your family live?

Phrase Bank

Telling the time
Unit 2
He wakes up at 8:00 a.m.
I go to school at six forty-five.
I usually get home at around six fifteen p.m.

Jobs
Unit 3
What do you do?
What's your job?
Where are you working?
I'm a …

Actions in progress
Unit 3
What are you doing (at the moment)?
I'm watching TV.
Nothing special.
Are you coming for coffee?
Where are you going?

Feelings
Unit 3
I'm not hungry.
I'm thirsty.

Offers
Unit 3
Do you want / Would you like a chocolate cookie?
No, thanks. I don't like them.
Do you want to watch TV?
Would you like a drink?
Yes, please. Black coffee, no sugar.
Would you like to go out?

On the phone
Unit 3
Hi. This is Maddie.
Are you busy?
Actually, yes, I'm cooking dinner.
Yes, I am. / Not really, I'm fine.
Can I call you later?
I can't hear you. Bye!
Meet you at the subway station? Let's go!
My battery's dying.
Nice talking to you.
No problem.
Sorry, wrong number.
Talk to you later.
The line's busy.

Weather and months
Unit 3
How's the weather in Chicago?
It's usually very rainy.
What's the temperature today?
It's about twenty-eight degrees.
What's the weather usually like there?
It's really hot and sunny.
What's your favorite month / season?
My birthday is in March.

Giving reasons
Unit 3
Why are you learning English?
Because I like it. / For pleasure.
For my job / school / college.
I have to pass an exam.
I need to write emails at work. / To communicate with people (face to face).
I want to travel / emigrate.
Why not?

Can
Unit 4
Can you run two kilometers?
I can, but not very well.
No, I can't. Not at all.
Yes, I can. Well, I think so.
I can speak two other languages.

Phrase Bank

Clothes

Unit 4
What's he wearing?
He's wearing black shorts and an old T-shirt.
Whose sweater is this? Is it yours?
No, it's not mine.
I have about twenty pairs of jeans.

Shopping

Unit 4
Can I help you?
Can I see those boots?
What color?
We have them in black or brown.
Black, please.
What size?
Can I try them on?
The fitting rooms are over there.
How much is it / are they?
Here's my credit card.
Please, enter your PIN number.
Here you are. / There you go.
Here's your receipt.
Have a nice day.

Sports

Unit 4
I don't / can't play baseball.
I go surfing every weekend.
My friends play soccer every weekend.
Our country is (usually) good at judo.

Directions

Unit 5
Are there any banks near here?
Do you know where the mall is?
Yes, go straight and turn right / left at the stoplight.
Is there a movie theater around here?
Yes, it's on Market Street.
Where's the bookstore?

Instructions

Unit 5
Don't forget to close the windows.
Please, feed my cat and my dog.
Remember to water the plants.

Other useful expressions

Unit 1
Are those / these your keys?
These are her keys.
This is my pen.
Can you say that again, please?
Don't worry about it.
Excuse me.
How do you spell ... / that?
I don't understand.
I'm online with my boyfriend.
Is that hotel in Spain?
Is that your bag?
Me, too.
Oh, sorry. / I'm sorry.
Sure ...
What are these in English?
They're windows.
It's a door.
This is my friend, Lucas.
What's the opposite of strong?
What are these?
What's that?
Yes, it is. / No, it isn't. It's in Mexico.
Yes, they are. / No, they aren't.
You're welcome.

Unit 2
What day is it today?
What do you usually do at Christmas?
Happy birthday!
Congratulations!
Enjoy your meal!
Happy New Year!
Have a good trip!
Merry Christmas!

Unit 3
Who's that?
What does she do?
She's a singer?

Unit 4
I love to go to salons.
I like to watch my team win.
My closet is small but clean and organized.

Phrase Bank

Invitations
Unit 7
Are you free on Friday?
Do you want to come to a barbecue?
I'm sorry. I already have plans.
How about going to a movie tonight?
Sure. That sounds good. / Sounds great.
I'm having a party on Saturday. Can you come?
Of course I can.
Sorry, I can't. But thanks for the invitation.
Maybe next time.
It's my birthday this week. Do you think you can come?
Sounds great! What can I bring? / What time?

Houses
Unit 7
In my opinion, a bed is absolutely essential.
This is the living room and that's the bathroom.

My town
Unit 7
There was(n't) a lot of traffic downtown.
There were / weren't a lot of malls / people.
Twenty years ago there was a park near my house.

Parties
Unit 7
What kind of party was it?
It was Jane's birthday party, at her house / home.
Was there a lot of food?
Yes, there was. / No, there wasn't.
Were Jane's parents there?
Yes, they were. / No, they weren't.

Past expressions
Unit 7
I was at a great party last month / yesterday evening.
It was awesome!
Were you (at) home last night?
Yes, I was, all evening.
Where were you (at 7 o'clock) yesterday morning?

Dates
Unit 8
My great grandmother was born on October 14th, 1861, and died on April 3rd, 1961.
Miley Cyrus was born in 1992, on November 23rd.

Favors
Unit 8
Could I ask you a favor? / Could you help me, please?
Could you do me a favor?
That depends. What do you want?
Could you open the door for me, please?
Sure. There you go.
Could you please do the dishes for me?
I'm (really) sorry, but I can't.
Come on, I can do it tomorrow.
OK. I'll do it now.
Don't worry, I'll get it.

Asking and giving permission
Unit 9
Can I ask you something?
Could I take the day off?
Can I take the car?
Could you lend me … ?
Do you mind if I turn off the air conditioning?
That's fine.
Sure. Go ahead.
Of course. No problem.
Help yourself.
Not at all.
No, I'm busy.
Maybe next time.
No, I'm sorry, you can't.
I'm sorry, but …
I'm sorry, but it's too cold.

Phones
Unit 8
Can I borrow your charger?
Can I use my phone? I left mine at home.
Can you tell me the Wi-Fi password, please?
I can't get a signal.
I can't talk right now can I call you later?

Phrase Bank

Reactions

Unit 8
That's fantastic!
That's incredible!
Oh no!
Wow!
You're kidding!
That's amazing!

Unit 10
Really? I didn't know that.
That sounds great. Problem solved!
That's terrible! Poor thing!

Vacations

Unit 8
Did you have a good time enjoy your vacation?
Yes, I did. It was great. / No, I didn't. It was …
How did you get there?
I went by car.
What did you do?
I went to the beach.
Who did you go with?
I went with my family.
What did you do last vacation?
What did you eat?
Where did you stay?

Food

Unit 6
My grandmother counts calories.
For breakfast I can only have a bottle of water.
I can't eat any meat. I'm a vegetarian.
I don't like oranges.
There was a special offer on bananas.
There's some milk in the refrigerator.
What do you have when you get up?
Yes, I can. But only a little.

In a restaurant

Unit 6
Would you like to see the menu?
Are you ready to order? / Can I take your order?
What would you like for your starter? / to start?
I'll have the soup, please.
Would you like to order the main course now?
I'd like the chicken, please.
(Can I get you) anything else?
No, that's all, thanks.
What would you like to drink?
Can I have a soda, please?
Can you bring us the check, please?
OK. Just a moment, please.
What do you have when you get up?
Yes, I can. But only a little.

Intentions

Unit 9
What are you going to do (when you finish school)?
I'm going to go to grad school.
I'm going to make a few changes.

Fixed future plans

Unit 9
After lunch he's meeting his teacher.
Tonight, he and his mother are having dinner.

Jobs

Unit 9
What do you do?
You can / can't make / earn a lot of money.
You help / don't help a lot of people.
You work alone / with other people.
I'm unemployed.
It's interesting / dangerous work.
You work / don't work long hours.
It's a job of the past / future.
It's a job I'd like / woulnd't like to do.

Transportation

Unit 9
How did you arrive here?
I came on foot.
How do you usually get to school / work?
I go by car. / I drive.
He rode his motorbike.

Phrase Bank

Describing people

Unit 10
Are you like your dad?
Do you look like your mom?
What is he / she like?
He's fun and spontaneous.
She has long dark hair.
She's short and slim and has brown eyes.
They're both energetic and very strong.
This person is tall with long, dark hair.
What color is her hair?
What does she look like?
What's he like?
Your sisters look identical!

Making comparisons

Unit 10
I'm more athletic than him, but he's taller.
I prefer Italian food, but it's more expensive.
Home is the nicest place in the world.
My writing is worse than my speaking.
Our apartment is bigger than Sheila's new house.
My dad is friendlier than I am. I'm a little shyer.

Making choices

Unit 10
Where do you want to go?
I can't decide where to go.
What do you recommend?
I'm not sure, but …
Why don't we go to the beach?
OK, let's go to the beach.

Other useful expressions

Unit 9
Great to see you!
I'm so pleased you came!
I never use elevators.
It isn't going to be easy.
That sounds boring / fun.
What happened?

Word List

This is a reference list. To check pronunciation of any individual words, you can use a talking dictionary.

Unit 1

Countries
Argentina
Brazil
Canada
Chile
China
Ecuador
India
Japan
Korea
Peru
Portugal
Spain
The UK
The U.S.

Nationalities
American
Argentinian
Brazilian
British
Canadian
Chilean
Chinese
Ecuadorian
Indian
Korean
Peruvian
Portuguese
Spanish

Opinion adjectives
amazing
cool
excellent
fantastic
horrible
important
intelligent
interesting
OK
rich
ridiculous
terrible

Numbers 11-100
11 eleven
12 twelve
13 thirteen
14 fourteen
15 fifteen
16 sixteen
17 seventeen
18 eighteen
19 nineteen
20 twenty
21 twenty-one
22 twenty-two
23 twenty-three
30 thirty
31 thirty-one
32 thirty-two
40 forty
41 forty-one
50 fifty
60 sixty
70 seventy
80 eighty
90 ninety
100 one hundred

Personal objects
a backpack
earrings
glasses
keys
a laptop / computer
a lipstick
a pencil
a phone
a sandwich
an umbrella
a wallet

Colors
blue
black
brown
green
orange
pink
purple
red
yellow

Adjectives
big
cheap
expensive
good
new
old
real
small
strong
weak
young

Unit 2

Places
café
church
gym
grocery store
home
party
school
work

Days of the week
Monday
Tuesday
Wednesday
Thursday
Friday
Saturday
Sunday

Morning routine
brush my teeth
exercise
get dressed
get up
have breakfast
leave home
make the bed
shave
take a shower
wake up

Family members
aunt
boyfriend
brother
child(ren)
couple
cousin(s)
daughter
father
girlfriend
grandfather
grandmother
grandparent(s)
husband
mother
nephew
niece
parent(s)
partner
sibling(s)
sister
son
twin(s)
uncle
wife

Frequency adverbs
always
usually
often
sometimes
occasionally
never

Holidays
Carnival
Christmas
Day of the Dead
New Year ('s Eve)

Unit 3

Weather words
Nouns
cloud
fog
rain
snow
sun
wind

Adjectives
cloudy
foggy
rainy
snowy
sunny
windy

Temperature
cold
cool
hot
warm

Months
January
February
March
April
May
June
July
August
September
October
November
December

Seasons
fall
spring
summer
winter

Unit 4

Sports
baseball
basketball
bike riding (cycling)
football
golf
handball
hockey
martial arts
rugby
running
skateboarding
skiing
soccer
surfing
swimming
(table) tennis
volleyball

Professions
babysitter
journalist
secretary
teacher

Clothes items
belt
blouse
boots
dress
jacket
pants
sandals
shirt
shoes
shorts
skirt
sneakers
socks
suit
sweater
tie
T-shirt

Unit 5

Places around town
bar
bookstore
bridge
club
hotel
library
mall
movie theater
museum
park
racetrack
restaurant
river
stadium
swimming pool
theater

Vacation activities
buying souvenirs
camping
cooking
dancing
eating out
hiking

Word List

kayaking
reading novels
sightseeing
snorkeling
sunbathing
swimming
taking a class
visiting museums

House sitting
don't let the cat out
feed the cat / dog
give the cat some water
open / close the windows
pick up / put the mail on the table
turn on / off the lights
walk the dog
water the plants

Adjectives
boring
cheap
dangerous
expensive
fun
messy
neat
safe

Unit 6

Food and drink
apple
banana
beans
bread
butter
cake
candy
carrot
cheese
chicken
chocolate
coconut water
coffee
cream
egg
fish
fries
fruit
grapes
ice
ice cream
juice
kiwi
lemonade
lettuce
mango
meat
melon
milk
nuts
oil
onion
orange (juice)
pasta
pear
pepper
pizza
potato
rice
salad
salt
soup
spaghetti
spinach

sports drink
steak
strawberry
sugar
tea
tofu
tomato
vegetables
vinegar
water
yogurt

Unit 7

Parts of the house
basement
bathroom
bedroom
dining room
garage
kitchen
laundry room
living room
office

Furniture
armchair
bathtub
bed
chair
closet
fan
fireplace
microwave
oven
refrigerator
shelves
shower
sink
sofa
stairs
storage space
stove
table
toilet
TV
window

Party items
balloons
birthday cards
cake
candles
coffee
glasses
invitations
juice
napkins
plates
presents
snacks
soft drinks
tea
water

Adjectives to describe places and events
amazing
awesome
beautiful
cold
fabulous
fantastic
magical
special
terrific
wonderful

Unit 8

Ordinal numbers
1st first
2nd second
3rd third
4th fourth
5th fifth
6th sixth
7th seventh
8th eighth
9th ninth
10th tenth
11th eleventh
12th twelfth
13th thirteenth
14th fourteenth
15th fifteenth
16th sixteenth
17th seventeenth
18th eighteenth
19th nineteenth
20th twentieth

Unit 9

Transportation
bike
bus
car
ferry
helicopter
motorbike
on foot
plane
train
truck

Professions
civil engineer
computer programmer
cook
dentist
designer
financial advisor
firefighter
flight attendant
hairdresser
market research analyst
nurse
optician
personal assistant
photographer
police officer
software developer
student

Life changes
find a girl/boyfriend
get engaged
get divorced
get married
leave college
leave home
lose a job
move
start a (new) job
start a family
retire (from a job)

Unit 10

The body and the face
arm
back
chest
ears
eyebrows
eyes
fingers
foot / feet
hair
hand
head
leg
lips
mouth
nose
stomach
teeth
toes

Description words and phrases
average build
average height
overweight
short
slim
tall

Adjectives
active
ambitious
angry
arrogant
athletic
bad
calm
courageous
critical
depressed
determined
disorganized
energetic
extraordinary
friendly
generous
happy
hard
heroic
idealistic
loyal
moody
nice
ordinary
passive
perfectionist
possessive
relaxed
responsible
romantic
sad
solitary
spontaneous
strong
suspicious

Geographical features
canyon
cave
forest
island
lake
mountain
river
rock
underground river
volcano
waterfall

Richmond

58 St Aldates
Oxford
OX1 1ST
United Kingdom

ISBN: 978-84-668-3055-3
First reprint: June 2019
CP: 944428

© Richmond / Santillana Global S.L. 2019

Publishing Director: Deborah Tricker
Publishers: Luke Baxter, Laura Miranda
Media Publisher: Luke Baxter
Editors: Sarah Curtis
Proofreaders: Lily Khambata, Diyan Leake, Rachael Williamson
Design Manager: Lorna Heaslip
Cover Design: Lorna Heaslip
Design & Layout: Rob Briggs, ROARR Design
Photo Researcher: Magdalena Mayo
Audio Production: John Marshall Media Inc.

We would like to thank all those who have given their kind permission to reproduce material for this book:

Illustrators: Alexandre Matos, Andrew Pagram, Vicente Mendonça

Photos:
J. Jaime; 123RF/Fabrizio Troiani, brulove, Tatiana Popova; ALAMY/Steve Skjold, Michey, Skyscan Photolibrary, Image Source Plus, Erwin Zueger, Dmitry Melnikov, AF Archive, Elena Elisseeva, Zoonar GmbH, F1online digitale Bildagentur GmbH; GETTY IMAGES SALES SPAIN/RB, Liam Norris, SolStock, JoKMedia, Paul Bradbury, By Vesi_127, Floortje, Kupicoo, Steve Granitz, Hackisan, Hero Images, Nattrass, Thomas Francois, Antonello, Drbimages, Electravk, NetaDegany, DigiStu, D-Keine, Photoservice, Gofotograf, Subjug, David Lees, MarianVejcik, Rob Kroenert, Gradyreese, Karaandaev, Kojihirano, G-stockstudio, NicoElNino, Thinkstock, Zak Kendal, Altayb, Donvictorio, Georgeclerk, Guenterguni, Jeff Greenberg, John Rowley, JohnnyGreig, Kevin Mazur, David Livingston, OksanaKiian, Philipphoto, Roger Kisby, Sam Edwards, Taylor Hill, Xavierarnau, 10'000 Hours, Morsa Images, Kevin Mazur/Billboard Awards 2014, Chris Ryan,

All rights reserved. No part of this book may be reproduced, stored in a retrieval system or transmitted in any form by any means, electronic, mechanical, photocopying, recording or otherwise, without the prior permission in writing of the Publisher.

Westend61, Image Source, IakovKalinin, Phil Fisk, Diana Miller, Ismailciydem, Kali9, Liesel Bockl, MachineHeadz, Deepblue4you, Mike Kemp, Noel Vasquez, PeopleImages, Dcdr, David Buchan, Sezeryadigar, South_agency, Tim Robberts, Caroline Sale, Chris Clinton, Fiona Goodall, Dave J Hogan, James Devaney, Jamie Garbutt, Jeffrey Mayer, Johner Images, Jupiterimages, Michael Kovac, Oliver Furrer, Istetiana, China Photos, Terry O'Neill, Yasser Chalid, Anthony Harvey, Cecilie_Arcurs, Hulton Archive, Ida Mae Astute, Axelle/Bauer-Griffin, LauriPatterson, Marc Romanelli, Martin Hospach, Newstockimages, JGI/Jamie Grill, Photos.com Plus, Stefanie Grewel, Victor Ovies Arenas, Andrew Merry, Jay L. Clendenin, Jeffrey Richards, Gareth Cattermole, Gonzalo Marroquin, Jonathan Paciullo, Oktay Ortakcioglu, RightFieldStudios, Robyn Breen Shinn, istock/Thinkstock, Stanton J Stephens, DEA / G. NIMATALLAH, Dave and Les Jacobs, Rajibul Hasan/EyeEm, Teresa Recena/EyeEm, Ian Gavan, Imv, BJI/Blue Jean Images, Caiaimage/Tom Merton, Gints Ivuskans/EyeEm, Jose Luis Pelaez Inc, Monkeybusinessimages, Tim Clayton - Corbis, Caiaimage/Sam Edwards, Dan Thornberg / EyeEm, Mendowong Photography, Science Photo Library, Tatiana Dyuvbanova/EyeEm, Jules Frazier Photography, Universal History Archive, Dennis Fischer Photography, Simpson33, Julia Finney; ISTOCKPHOTO/Getty Images Sales Spain; SHUTTERSTOCK/ Kseniia Perminova, threerocksimages, Sergey Peterman, Ilya Sviridenko, PhotoHouse, eurobanks, AJR_photo, hxdbzxy, kurhan; ARCHIVO SANTILLANA

The Publisher has made every effort to trace the owner of copyright material; however, the Publisher will correct any involuntary omission at the earliest opportunity.

Printed in Mexico by Litografica Ingramex, S.A. de C.V., Centeno 162-1, Col. Granjas Esmeralda, C.P. 09810, Ciudad de México